Your Privacy on the Internet

Everything you need to know about
protecting your privacy and security online

11/05

GW00569731

Internet Handbooks

1001 Web Sites for Writers on the Internet
Books and Publishing on the Internet
Building a Web Site on the Internet
Careers Guidance on the Internet
Chat & Chat Rooms on the Internet
Creating a Home Page on the Internet
Discussion Forums on the Internet
Finding a Job on the Internet
Getting Started on the Internet
Gardens & Gardening on the Internet
Graduate Job Hunting on the Internet
Homes & Property on the Internet
Human Resource Management on the Internet
Internet Explorer on the Internet
Internet for Schools
Internet for Students
Internet for Writers
Law & Lawyers on the Internet
Linking Your Web Site on the Internet
Marketing Your Business on the Internet
Music & Musicians on the Internet
Naming a Web Site on the Internet
News and Magazines on the Internet
Overseas Job Hunting on the Internet
Personal Finance on the Internet
Promoting a Web Site on the Internet
Protecting Children on the Internet
Shops & Shopping on the Internet
Studying English on the Internet
Studying Law on the Internet
Travel & Holidays on the Internet
Using Credit Cards on the Internet
Using Email on the Internet
Using Netscape on the Internet
Where to Find It on the Internet
Wildlife & Conservation on the Internet
Working from Home on the Internet
Your Privacy on the Internet

Many other titles in preparation

Your Privacy
on the internet

Everything you need to know about
protecting your privacy and security online

Kye Valongo

www.internet-handbooks.co.uk

Other Internet Handbooks by the same author

Discussion Forums on the Internet
Getting Started on the Internet
Internet Explorer on the Internet
Using Email on the Internet
Using Netscape on the Internet
Where to Find It on the Internet

Acknowledgements

Thanks to helpful netizens wherever you may be. I know you only by your emails and usenet posts, but you are all beautiful.

First published in 2000 by Internet Handbooks, a Division of International Briefings Ltd, Plymbridge House, Estover Road, Plymouth PL6 7PY, United Kingdom.

Customer services tel:	(01752) 202301
Orders fax:	(01752) 202333
Customer services email:	cservs@plymbridge.com
Distributors web site:	www.plymbridge.com
Internet Handbooks web site:	www.internet-handbooks.co.uk

Note: The contents of this book are offered for the purposes of general guidance only and no liability can be accepted for any loss or expense incurred as a result of relying in particular circumstances on statements made in this book. Readers are advised to check the current position with the appropriate authorities before entering into personal arrangements.

Case studies in this book are entirely fictional and any resemblance to real persons or organisations is entirely coincidental.

Typeset in Monotype Univers by PDQ Typesetting, Newcastle-under-Lyme
Printed and bound by The Cromwell Press Ltd, Trowbridge, Wiltshire.

Contents

Contents..

List of illustrations

Introduction: The new internet street war

It is a popular misconception that our home is our castle. Unfortunately, castles are not what they used to be. Today they are suffering from neglect, and many have crumbled to the point where they are unable to fend off even the most harmless invader.

Our privacy has deteriorated to a similar state – especially on the internet. Hidden eyes spy on us from almost every angle imaginable. Some of the threats to personal privacy go as unnoticed as the microscopic mites that share our beds. Others openly demand the power to tear down our door and empty the whole place, leaving only the safe – which is empty because 'they' have taken the combination away from us.

In this alarming new information age, you will need to learn how to defend your own privacy. Do you need protection? Most certainly. The revelation of private information can leave you vulnerable in many ways. Private information such as your email address, telephone number and postal address, once obtained can ultimately weaken your ability to protect yourself and your family. And that is only the start. You need protection as a citizen, as a saver and investor, as a parent, consumer, employee and medical patient let alone as a dissident, journalist, student activist or member of a threatened social minority.

Some will say that the law will protect us, but that is less and less true. The authorities pursue law breakers and those who flout regulation, but they cannot mount guard on everyone 24 hours a day.

▶ *Example 1* – your daughter joins a children's chat room and makes a friend called Lucy. Lucy and her have struck up such a good friendship online that they agree to meet in real life. Lucy says she has been hurt by her parents and so insists that your daughter be alone when they meet. Lucy turns out to be a forty-year-old male paedophile. Your privacy and security are *very* much at risk.

▶ *Example 2* – Your children have moved to secondary school and seem to be mixing with bad company. One weekend, you decide to surf the web and look up information on drugs, worried that your children may come in contact with local pushers. You find some useful sites and some others that look very strange. You buy a book from an online bookshop on the effects of illegal drugs, and you sign up for a newsletter run by reformed drug addicts to help others. Your activities are logged by large marketing companies. At work, your yearly review comes round and you are asked some pointed questions about drugs and find that your promotion has been postponed for a year. Why? Because your personnel department paid cash for your profile from one of the marketing companies and assumed that you had a problem yourself.

Democratic governments claim to have the interest of their people at heart, but it is a mistake to rely solely on them to protect you. Government leaders may have very different motives for wanting to erode their citizens' privacy. Many a politician has used underhand techniques to squash opposition and dissent. In some countries, disagreeing with the government results in harassment and persecution. Do you think it doesn't happen in your own country? Often the facts only come to light years later.

Although loud protests are being voiced about the threat of government eavesdropping, governments are in reality overworked and out of their depth. They are drowning in the floods of their own legislation. They are years behind the other, more motivated, threats out there: big business and the internet 'outlaws'.

We see many large and 'respectable' companies in a mad rush to start trading on the internet but few of them are making a profit. The rush is not for immediate profit but for the gold dust of information — information about you and every scrap of it they can get. This is a privacy violation, and a risk to your security. Information is power, and information about you gives people power over you. Businesses are, ultimately, after one thing: your money. The more information they have on you, the more they can manipulate you with custom-made promises and threats, and part you from your money — not unlike politicians, perhaps, who for years have similarly used a mixture of promises and threats to make citizens part with their votes.

'Cyber criminals' may also want to part you from your money, though many get their biggest kick out of being malicious. Cyber crime is not as widespread a threat as big business, but when cyber criminals do strike the damage inflicted can be far more severe. After all, they do not stick to legal methods of manipulation or attack. The loss of your personal or financial privacy online could be catastrophic.

Neither your government, nor criminals, nor marketing companies, are going to admit to spying on you — but rest assured they are, and devoting enormous sums of money to doing so. When using the internet, you are as weak and exposed as a lone lamb on a bare hillside. Protecting your privacy and security on the internet is like dealing with outlaws during the Gold Rush before the sheriff came to town. The incredible growth of internet technology and activity far outpaces the ability of any government or consumer organisation to protect us.

Even if regulations could be effectively enforced, the internet is so overwhelming that the enforcers will be ever more hard-pressed to deal with all the new threats. Your defence has to come from you. The good news is that you can use technology, too. You can learn to protect yourself effectively so that no agency, business or criminal will be able to break through — unless you let them.

A reporter in Prishtina, Kosovo, released a report on the fighting just after being evicted from her home thanks to the internet and its ability to protect her from the Yugoslav government. Reporters all over the world are using the internet to report on some of the worst atrocities of this century in some of the most repressive countries.

While you are unlikely to attract an attack from the Yugoslav government, you may be the subject of lesser, but still disturbing, attacks. This book will describe effective ways to protect yourself against many forms of intrusion, from the small bugs that track your movements by infesting your hard disk, to unwarranted government monitoring; from the colleague who 'borrows' your password to the growing menaces of the cyberstalker and professional identity-thief.

The question many people ask is, 'If I have nothing to hide why should I need privacy?' Then are you prepared to let your government or big business open your letters, or listen in to your telephone conversations? Would you be willing to permanently deposit a copy of your front door key with the police, or with the tax officials? Are you willing for unknown local or foreign companies to obtain your online passwords, user identities, bank balance, investment, legal and health records – and to trade that information among themselves? Few people would answer yes. Today, on the internet, organisations of all kinds are investing literally billions to monitor you without your knowledge. The information they collect is held in huge databases and sold to anyone who wants it. You don't have to be a terrorist to be under surveillance today. If you surf the web, *you* are under surveillance.

The internet is the most extraordinary phenomenon to enter human life for generations. The unprecedented power of technology, and impact of rapid globalisation, is going to shake to their very foundations all the national institutions and ways of life we have taken for granted for so long.

Kye Valongo

kvalongo@internet-handbooks.co.uk

Your privacy checklist

Do you mind if:

▶ All kinds of government agencies monitor your emails and web logs.

▶ Your internet service provider builds a record of your browsing habits.

▶ Staff at your internet service provider read your unencoded emails.

▶ A web site ignores its 'privacy policy' and sells your details.

▶ Web sites build up records of your surfing habits without your knowledge.

▶ Insurance firms trade your personal, financial and health records over the internet.

▶ Your ISP refuses to answer your questions about your privacy online.

▶ The tax authorities monitor the financial web sites you visit.

▶ The Department of Social Security knows what job sites you visit.

▶ The health services acquire data about your drinking, smoking and dietary preferences.

▶ Your spouse reads the emails you sent to your accountant or lawyer.

▶ Your email 'inbox' gets saturated with spam.

▶ The police are given powers to read emails at random without a warrant.

▶ Your online bank activity is subject to government surveillance.

▶ Cookies are written to your hard drive, tracking your visits to web sites.

▶ Your children discover your passwords or read your 'deleted' emails.

▶ Someone at your workplace monitors your key-word searches and web-site visits.

▶ You can never truly delete a file on your computer.

▶ Records which you can never challenge are accumulated about you on the net.

▶ The government demands a copy of all your passwords.

If you've nothing to hide, you have nothing to fear (... *have you?*)

Part One: The threats

. . . .

▶ *Privacy* - 'Privacy is the ability to control what, when and how your personal data is given to other people. Powerful institutions believe their right to privacy has a bona fide basis (for instance, 'national security' or 'trade secrets'), while the individual's claim to privacy is suspicious and subject to these institutions' veto. For me, privacy is a necessary part of democracy. That's why we vote with secret ballots.' (Andre Bacard, *The Computer Privacy Handbook*).

With normal telephone conversations, you can find a private place to talk and the conversation is over once you hang up the telephone. The internet is different. You leave a trail behind you that can last many months or even years. Others can read your email messages, they can trace your surfing habits, and the posts you make to newsgroup will be stored, and some may even be published in books or on web sites.

Privacy is a complex issue and may not be resolved for years, if ever. But one thing is for certain once our privacy has been violated, it is almost impossible to reverse the damage. To defend yourself, you first need to understand and identify the threats.

Threats to privacy come from all directions. It's not always an onslaught but often a random barrage of pushy initiatives that just happen to be coming together. They form an alliance of information systems with the potential to hold frightening amounts of information on each one of us. The danger is that each of the threats seems justifiable when viewed alone, but when they start to link up, and they are, your privacy will be eroded to such an extent that there will be little that is not known about you. From your shoe size to your sexual orientation or religious values all of it will be there for anyone to use.

Sometimes we can build up a false sense of privacy. On Usenet, for example, we may exchange messages merrily discussing our carelessly worded opinions on our employers or lover believing that the group is only read by a trusted few. It is only later, when we are fired for libelling the company, or wake up in an empty bed, we realise that the group was far from a safe place to talk.

Your email

Is email private then? No, once you send a message, it can be read by anyone who has the ability to intercept it. This includes anyone with access to any of the computer systems that your message is relayed through (which can be anywhere in the world at any time) and hackers who know how to enter those systems by stealth.

In fact the internet as a whole is unsafe. It is a vast network of computers including yours once you are connected. Each time you send a message or browse the web, you are connecting with a chain of computers in countries scattered around the world. It only takes one of the links in this chain to become corrupt and your privacy is gone. Our defences must, therefore, be numerous and varied to deal with the different types of threat.

But first of all, what are the threats?

1 Big Brother and you

In this chapter we will explore:

▶ *internet eavesdropping and surveillance*

▶ *who is accountable for the internet?*

▶ *the internet, the individual, and the power of the State*

▶ *your internet service provider and your personal privacy*

▶ *Enfopol and Echelon: what you should know*

▶ *the biggest threat to yourself is – you*

▶ *case studies*

. . . .

Internet eavesdropping and surveillance

How much are we watched over and followed as we go about our business on the internet? The full extent may never be known, but what *is* known will be enough to give any right-thinking person a nasty shiver each time he or she sends an email message or posts a message to a Usenet newsgroup.

The internet is an immensely powerful tool for eavesdropping and finding information about individual people. Just by monitoring a person's Usenet posts, you can find out a great deal about their habits, opinions and weaknesses. That information can then be used for commercial, criminal and law-enforcement purposes. Police forces and criminals alike can keep tabs on you simply and legally by using search engines. There are no search warrants to obtain or noisy crowbars to bother with – monitoring someone's internet activities is as simple as clicking a mouse button.

If you have rich tastes or dissident views, you should learn about the defence techniques in this book. Learn how to encrypt your messages, and how to detect the bugs on your computer that track your movements for the benefit of unseen others.

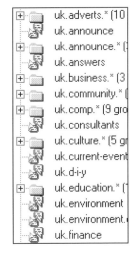

▶ *Usenet* – a network of special interest forums or discussion groups (tens of thousands) called newsgroups.

▶ *Newsgroup* – a Usenet discussion group that is similar to a notice board. You can 'post' a message or reply to another's message. Often a series of posts and replies (a 'thread') can develop into many separate offshoot discussions started by the one original post.

Each time you connect onto the internet, you will be tracked by dozens of different web sites, companies and organisations. Web sites spend serious money secretly tracking your activities, and many of them team up and pool their knowledge of you to compile detailed dossiers. Your only real hope of maintaining your privacy lies in common sense, discretion and the use of good security technologies as described in this book.

Who is accountable for the internet?

There are about 200 governments in the world. Some of them exert total and frightening control over their people, and little of what they do is known or accounted for. For them, the internet is a valuable new surveillance tool. Most democratic governments – despite appearing to be acting in the name of the people – pour immense resources into eavesdropping on the internet communications of ordinary people. Furthermore, thousands of government employees have access to the information obtained, and you can be sure that some will abuse it.

Fig. 1. The UK and US governments have jointly and secretly developed an enormously powerful surveillance system called Echelon. This constantly monitors emails, phone calls, fax messages and other electronic communications. Echelon Watch aims to tell the public what is going on.

We happily assume that governments usually have the good of their citizens in mind as they govern. But it is clear today that many countries give preferential treatment to the internationally rich and powerful, yet use increasingly draconian methods to control, regulate and tax the rest of their people.

The people of one country may even be largely controlled by a foreign government. For example, the USA is gaining ever more influence in the affairs of other countries. Even in the UK, it is allowed (by the UK government) to snoop on all 'private' electronic communications such as fax, email, and telephone conversations (see Echelon on page 22). They do this round the clock, without any need to account to the UK government let alone to you as a citizen.

The internet, the individual and the State

However, the internet is providing a great challenge to heavy-handed government. The internet is proving impossible to control. It is a self-organising society in itself without any centralised government. The people on the net organise themselves, police themselves, read what they like, form their own opinions, say what they like and do business without the bureaucratic control we endure in real life. In 1995, Ian Taylor, Britain's technology minister, admitted that it is virtually impossible for governments to control the internet. But that does not stop them trying. They frighten the public with talk about drug dealers, paedophiles and terrorists using the internet but is that really their main agenda?

The Electronic Communications Bill
At the time of writing (2000), the Labour government introduced the Regulation of Investigatory Powers Bill. This initally included a section that could put you in prison for two years if you failed to provide your encryption keys to law enforcement agencies whenever demanded. Appallingly, it attempted to introduce into UK law for the first time the presumption of guilt until proved innocent. Additionally, anyone telling customers about their accounts being tapped (your internet service provider for example) could face five years in prison.

▶ *Encryption* – the scrambling of information to make it unreadable without a personal key or password.

▶ *Internet service provider (ISP)* – the company that enables you to access the internet. They usually also provide you with internet software and other online services.

Cyber-Rights and Cyber-Liberties (UK), a leading UK privacy rights group, claimed that the new legislation infringes civil liberties and threatens the development of internet commerce within the UK. The campaigning group says that users should be required to decrypt messages for the police, if there is sufficient reason – but not to hand over their private key. An appropriate amendment was subsequently added.

Dr Brian Gladman, technical policy advisor at Cyber-Rights and Cyber-Liberties, said: 'Honest citizens may have been forced to hand over keys on which their security and privacy depended. Worse still, they could even have been imprisoned for withholding a key that they never had and knew nothing whatsoever about'. Gladman added that the proposals were also likely to undermine confidence in electronic commerce instead of promoting its rapid development.

CYBER-RIGHTS & CYBER-LIBERTIES (UK)
A Non Profit Civil Liberties Organisation
<http://www.cyber-rights.org>

Big Brother and you ....

home

demo

features

download

propaganda

pricing

Adi Shamir, an Israeli scientist, suggested that letting a government or agency keep only a part of the key would allow software companies to include strong cryptography into their products without denying law enforcement. The length of the part of the key kept by the user could vary – based on what is currently considered hard to break. Over time, as techniques improve, the length of the private part of the key would need to grow.

Partial surrendering of the key could be the least controversial method of what is called key escrow. That is, a company or individual could act as their own escrow agent (keeper of the keys). If a key is lost, the company could consult its own escrow and reduce the recovery work.

Many people are opposed to government enforcement of key escrow because it would tend to destroy the free market.

▶ *Key escrow* – A system in which people's encryption keys would be kept 'secure' by an escrow agency. Unfortunately, the keys would have to be made available to the authorities any time on demand, so the 'security' is non-existent.

Interception of Communications Act (IOCA)

In 1999 interception of email in the UK was granted only with a signature from the Secretary of State if the ISP is registered as a public telecommunications provider, such as Demon Internet and BT Internet. Police access to email messages stored by other ISPs (mainly the free ISPs) could not be enforced. The ISP would need to agree to the interception. New proposals would formalise these arrangements in law and allow the police to prosecute ISPs who refuse to comply.

The new proposals will expand the powers of the British government to:

1. include interception of internet communications
2. include all communications relating to a particular person
3. allow people other than the Secretary of State to authorise interception
4. include all UK-based ISPs
5. extend the period for interception from two months to between three and six months, including private business and other networks
6. force UK-based ISPs to hand over private data to the authorities, without any need for a court order

In anticipation of the bill, the government is planning to set up an eavesdropping facility, called the Government Technical Assistance Centre, capable of tracking every email and internet hit in the country (see page 17). The law will force ISPs to install equipment so that law enforcement organisations can intercept email and other internet communications at will.

▶ 'There are serious concerns for ISPs,' said Yaman Akdeniz, director of Cyber-Rights and Cyber-Liberties. 'It will be an intrusive system for their businesses, and the cost factor could push small-scale ISPs out of business. That's not good for the development of the internet or ecommerce.' Government policy officers and ministers will now draft the legislation, but the Home Office said it could not estimate when the bill will be debated.

GCHQ and other monitoring institutions

A government official told London newspaper *Metro* that major criminal organisations (especially drugs cartels) were extremely sophisticated. 'They have whole departments working on codes so they can carry on business in secret,' he said. 'For now the encryption problem is not huge but it is going to grow and we need to be ready for it.' In 1996 and 1997, authorised phone tapping operations in the UK resulted in 1,200 arrests and the seizure of 450 firearms and 115 tons of narcotics. There is no doubt that monitoring organisations catch criminals – but is this all they do?

No, it is not. In June 1992, *The Observer* newspaper published statements from a group of 'highly placed intelligence operatives' from GCHQ. They said: 'We feel we can no longer remain silent regarding that which we regard to be gross malpractice and negligence within the establishment in which we operate.' They gave, as examples, GCHQ interception of Amnesty International and Christian Aid. *The Observer* reported: 'At any time, GCHQ is able to home in on their communications for a routine target request.' The full extent of eaves-dropping on the public is not known, but leaks have increasingly appeared in the wall of government secrecy, and yield alarming clues.

The Government Telecommunications Advisory Centre

The creation of a new unit may mean that internet eavesdropping becomes far more common. In September 1999, *The Register*[1] reported

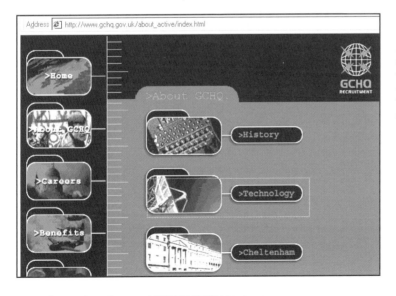

Address http://www.gchq.gov.uk/about_active/index.html

>Home

>About GCHQ

>History

>Technology

>Careers

>Benefits

>Cheltenham

GCHQ RECRUITMENT

Fig. 3. Based in Cheltenham, UK, GCHQ is another top-secret government organisation that constantly monitors electronic communications between the UK and other countries.

1. http://www.theregister.co.uk/990906-000014.html

Big Brother and you ....

that the UK government was setting up a unit of professional code crackers to track drug runners and paedophile rings on the internet. The unit will get between £20 to 40 million in government funding. It will be staffed by encryption specialists from GCHQ, as well as new recruits from the private sector. It is expected to be called the Government Telecommunications Advisory Centre (GTAC). In essence, GTAC will be an extension of government surveillance. The National Criminal Intelligence Service provides staff and support for GTAC.

National Security Agency (NSA) and the clipper chip

The American National Security Agency is the USA's spy agency. In 1993, it introduced the clipper chip. This was a hardware method of encrypting communications that would be built into all computers. The chip would be manufactured with a legal requirement forcing users to make their decoding keys available for storage in a central database accessible to government agencies. It would be just like leaving your front door key with the police, in case they needed to get into your house 'while you were away'. In the face of overwhelming opposition from internet and civil liberties groups, the plan was scrapped.

Fig. 4. This Techweb news report refers to the alleged 'back door' people say that Microsoft has placed in its software, so that the US National Security Agency (NSA) can easily gain access to people's computers.

The NSA and Microsoft

Microsoft has a poor track record in computer security, but most of us can accept those problems and carry on with life. But how is a British IT manager to feel upon discovering that Microsoft may have installed a 'back door' in Windows security for the National Security Agency, to help the US government look inside their computers?

While checking the security aspects of Windows NT4, chief scientist

Andrew Fernandes came across what is believed to be a back door for the NSA in every copy of Windows operating systems. Normally, Windows components are stripped of identifying information. But in a part of Windows NT4, Microsoft seemed to have forgotten to remove the symbolic information identifying the security components. Fernandes claims to have found that there are really two keys used by Windows encryption; the first belongs to Microsoft, the second belongs to the NSA. That means that the NSA can also perform secure actions on your machine, without your authorisation or knowledge.

The result is that it is easier for the NSA to load unauthorised security devices on all copies of Microsoft Windows. Once these are loaded, they can apparently compromise your entire operating system. For non-Americans who need to rely on Windows software to work with secure data, this is extremely worrying. The US government has, in the past, made it as difficult as possible for strong cryptographic capabilities to be used outside of the USA. That they also seem to have installed a back-door into the world's most popular operating system should ring the alarm bells in every non-US organisation, throughout the private and public sectors.

Your internet service provider and your personal privacy

Besides various governments keeping track of you, your own ISP may be far from innocent. Most ISPs keep fairly extensive records of when and where their users log in, what they do while connected, and when they do it. This information is usually publicly available. The ISP has to take precautions against attackers, and one of the ways is to log all attempts to log into their system, including by you. How else would they identify and catch hackers and crackers?

▶ *Cracker* – Someone who breaks into computer systems with the intention of causing some kind of damage or abusing the system.

▶ *Hacker* – A person interested in computer programming, operating systems, the internet and computer security. The term can be used to describe a person who breaks into computer systems with the intention of pointing out the weaknesses in a system. In common usage, the term is often wrongly used to describe a cracker.

Most features of this logging process are enabled by default after the initial installation of an ISP's software. The ISP's staff can also customise it to increase or decrease the amount of monitoring. This information is often viewed for troubleshooting purposes and other reasons. The kind of information logged includes unsuccessful log-ins and other activities that the supervisor may find suspicious.

What your ISP may be doing
Here are some of the things that your 'friendly' ISP may be doing:

1. Compiling records of all the web sites you visit.

2. Noting the key words you type into search engines.

3. Selling the personal registration information that you gave them.

4. Providing logon software that uploads personal details about you to companies that have paid to track your activities.

5. Actively monitoring what you do in newsgroups and chat rooms.

6. Keeping copies of your email messages and attached files, both sent and received, even if your email software 'deletes it off the server'.

Your ISP's privacy policy

ISPs differ in how they use the information that they collect about you. The way to check on your ISP is first to look up its privacy policy. Here are some questions to ask yourself when reading it:

(a) Does your ISP ask unreasonably invasive questions in its registration form?

(b) Does your ISP tell you how the information about you is going to be used?

(c) Does your ISP disclose information about you to other companies?

(d) Does your ISP tell you what information is being collected about you, and why?

(e) Can you see for yourself the information that your ISP collects about you?

(f) Can you correct or update the information they have collected about you?

(g) What happens to your email when you 'delete' it from the server (i.e. from their computer)?

(h) Is your email address made available to other subscribers?

Fig. 5. An example of an online privacy policy (Virgin Net). All privacy policies should be read very carefully before you agree to reveal any personal information about yourself to a web site. There may well be times when a particular web site's 'privacy policy' will do you no good at all.

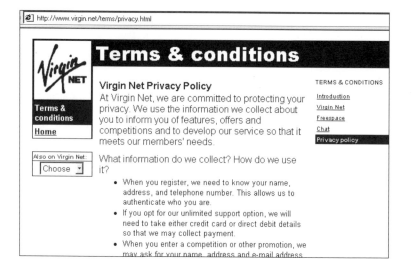

Fig. 6. *Wired News* reports on the domestic spying activities of the US National Security Agency (NSA).

(i) Have you any control over how your ISP uses its information about you?

Whatever you do, make sure that you look at the terms of service and privacy policies of whatever service you subscribe to – not only ISPs. If you are in any doubt, why not write to them and formally request them to answer your concerns?

Yahoo!
In July 1999, part of Yahoo!'s (a free ISP) terms of service said:

> 'By submitting content to any Yahoo! property, you automatically grant, or warrant that the owner of such content has expressly granted, Yahoo! the royalty-free, perpetual, irrevocable, non-exclusive and fully sublicensable right and license to use, reproduce, modify, adapt, publish, translate, create derivative works from, distribute, perform and display such content (in whole or part) worldwide and/or to incorporate it in other works in any form, media, or technology now known or later developed.'

In other words, whatever kind of material/messages went through their servers, they could use in absolutely any way they wanted. The reaction of users to this wording was a torrent of complaints and bad publicity so much so that Yahoo! has since made the wording less draconian.

ISP staff
The most serious threats from your ISP are immature or unscrupulous system operators, who may enjoy reading your mail while it is being transmitted. System administrators may also surreptitiously release your files to the police and other State agencies when asked – Inland

Revenue? Customs & Excise? Contributions Agency? Department of Health & Social Security? Child Support Agency? Passport Office? Department for Education & Employment? The procedure for revealing your information to outside agencies is still far from clear. It is worth knowing that whenever an email message is bounced, it will go back to the postmaster at a given site: if you address mail with an incorrect address it has a very good chance of being read by a human other than your intended recipient.

- **EnfoPol** Stopp
  ... **ENFOPOL** News
  ...http://www.quintes
  http://www.quintesse

- **Enfopol** Plans I
  ...Systran. Telepolis
  ...For months nothin
  http://www.cryptome

- **eCE archive:** FV
  ...Alternative to ECH
  ...Europe's Alternati
  http://www.dbai.tuwie

- **Big Brother is O**
  ...AGREEMENTS or
  http://echelon.tsx.or

- The **ENFOPOL**
  ...About.com networ

Enfopol and Echelon: what you should know

Enfopol: monitoring the internet

In 1999, European political leaders planned to introduce a global wiretapping system, Enfopol. This was to include the monitoring of people's emails and other internet communications. The European Council of Member States later abandoned the text of this particular proposal because of pressure from Britain and the Netherlands, and from industry bodies such as the European Internet Service Providers Association (EuroISPA). The original text would have allowed law enforcement agencies extensive access to communications on the internet. Opponents criticised the text for being vague and lacking in safeguards. Jean Christophe LeToquin, president of EuroISPA, said:

'The biggest flaw of the Enfopol proposal was that many of the points have not been clearly defined. The text calls for 'full time, real time access' to 'new' forms of communication, without even attempting to explain what exactly is or is not covered and who would pay for the surveillance.'

▶ *Update* – A complete rewrite of the Enfopol wiretapping proposals is again in progress.

Echelon: official internet spying agency

In the late 1980s, New Zealand joined a new coalition of countries[2] that monitored the activities of countries in the Pacific. Various staff members of the New Zealand's largest intelligence organisation, the Government Communications Security Bureau (GCSB), felt that some of these activities should be made public. The author Nicky Hager, in his book *Secret Power*, states that he interviewed more than 50 people in the New Zealand intelligence community.

One of the most important, and controversial, projects to come to light was called Echelon. Echelon indiscriminately intercepts huge quantities of communications, including email. It identifies messages of interest from a vast list of keywords and key phrases.

▶ *Note* – The emails you send and receive will under go this surveillance.

---

2. USA, UK, Australia, Canada and New Zealand.

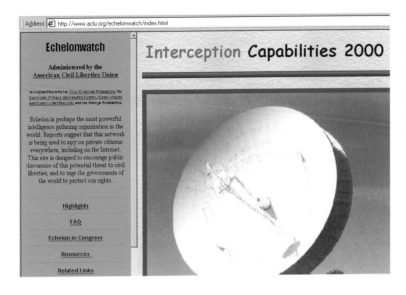

Fig. 7. Echelon Watch has published this picture of one of the numerous scanning dishes alleged to be used by the British government to eavesdrop on people's email and telephone conversations 24 hours a day.

Before Echelon, similar systems were used, but the keywords were compiled and controlled by the host country. With Echelon, each country's interception system, called a 'Dictionary', is linked in with the Dictionaries in the other member countries. Marked messages are sent not to the host country but to the agency and country concerned. So, if a message in New Zealand is intercepted and contains keywords of interest to a USA agency, it is sent direct to them and no one in the New Zealand agencies will even know about it.

The existence of these Dictionaries was exposed on Granada Television's *World in Action* in 1991 in an anonymous interview with a former GCHQ employee. The employee described a building in London at 8 Palmer Street, where GCHQ intercepted every telex that passed through London with a program called a 'Dictionary'. The system 'secretly intercepts every single telex which passes into, out of or through London; thousands of diplomatic, business and personal messages every day.' The programme pointed out that the Dictionary computers, although controlled by GCHQ, were operated by security staff at British Telecom. The presence of Dictionary computers has also been confirmed in Australia, and at GCHQ Cheltenham, England.

Your government is spying on you
Of course, you have nothing to hide. But are you prepared for your emails to be routinely intercepted and read by BT employees? Suppose you tell a friend about a great computer game (Delta Force) you are playing, or a book you have just read (John LeCarre), you will probably be monitored because you will be talking about drug barons, terrorists, planting bombs, and shooting people. The Echelon system will pick those words up; it will signal a human being who will then start reading your email, listening to your telephone conversations, and building a secret profile on you.

Big Brother and you ....

While some of these systems *seem* to be justified by the goal to catch criminals, the real baddies know about this technology, too – and are likely only to use innocent code words when communicating. 'The explosives are in my hotel room, I'll pick up the detonators at 5 p.m.,' Would probably be picked up by Echelon, but a veiled message would not be: 'The cake is at my place, I'll pick up the candles at 5.'

All email, telephone and fax communications are routinely intercepted by the United States National Security Agency, transferring selected information by Satellite to Fort Meade in Maryland via Menwith Hill in the North York Moors. This extraordinary site was first uncovered in the 1970s by a group of researchers.

Other work uncovered a billion-dollar world wide interceptions network, which was later found to be Echelon. Nicky Hager's book *Secret Power* (Hager, 1996) provides comprehensive details of Echelon. This global surveillance system listens in on all of the key satellites used to relay most of the world's satellite phone calls, internet, email, faxes and telexes.

▶ *Question* – If you are willing for your emails to be read by the State, are you prepared for all your letters to be opened and read by the State, as well?

Big Brother

What is the real goal of governments?
So, what is the real purpose of these surveillance networks? What do governments really want? To scan the phone networks for dissenting remarks? To listen in on conversations about tax havens and offshore strategies, and provide their details to tax or financial crime agencies for further investigation? (In the UK, tax investigations are set to rise by 50% in the new tax year.) To keep an eye on 'the opposition' like President Clinton's Democratic administration, which found itself with unauthorised secret dossiers on hundreds of Republican opponents in the 'Filegate' scandal? To spy on people out of work and claiming benefit? Is this now happening in Britain? Do you consider the following internet messages to be confidential:

1. emails to and from your accountant or solicitor?
2. self-assessment tax returns sent over the internet (as the Inland Revenue would like)?
3. emails applying for a job, your personal CV, and an employer's replies?
4. discussions about a business deal?
5. your online share transactions?
6. matters affecting your children?
7. your emails dealing with personal health matters?
8. your online banking transactions?

Is the purpose of this system to protect you from crime, or to protect the government from you? Have you been consulted? Is your right to privacy worth anything to you? Why has this surveillance been put in place now, while only a minority of the population so far use the internet? Big Brother – long ago imagined by George Orwell in his prophetic novel *1984* – may well turn out be Echelon and the UK government's surveillance system.

▶ *Important* – Never use email for any confidential discussion without using encryption or some form of prearranged code.

The biggest threat to yourself is – *you*

You are probably the biggest threat to your own privacy. In an age of heavy taxation and vast welfare states, we have grown accustomed to sit back and expect others to protect us whether it is the government or some other agency such as our ISP. We have forgotten how to protect ourselves, and lost the will to do so. The government seems to cover us with a warm blanket and protect us from the cold.

The internet is a whole new challenge for people all over the world, and the ways of the past are not likely to work in the future. On the one hand, we expect to be protected from undesirable invasions such as spam and email harassment. On the other, we want to protect our own privacy and freedom of speech. We want to have unrestricted access to information on the web, but at the same to time protect children from material we find offensive.

These ambiguities – combined with the speed of technological advance – mean that governments everywhere are in a difficult position: almost impotent. When governments try to legislate for illegal internet activity, they do so with sledgehammer proposals likely to cause more damage for law-abiding citizens than good.

It is time to learn how to defend yourself. With the help of the methods and tools described later in this book, you will learn how to 'police' your own internet experience far more successfully (and cheaply) than any government could.

The global nature of the internet means that heavy-handed national policing is doomed to fail. If carried to excess by ever more paranoid governments, it could even discourage ordinary people and businesses from wanting to use the internet at all.

Case studies

Encryption exports
In February 1995, Daniel Bernstein, a postgraduate student at the University of California, sued the American government. He challenged the law that classified encryption software as 'munitions' and restricted the export of those products. He claimed that the law was a violation of the first amendment to the American constitution, that of free speech. In May 1999 Bernstein, with the help of the EFF and many other sympathetic people, won the case – but the US politicians and bureaucrats are still dragging their feet.

Big Brother and you ....

Syria operates the internet

The Syrian Public Authority for Wired and Wireless Communication is now authorising access to the internet in Syria – as long as it is monitored. The monitoring relies on a central server controlled by the Syrian telephone authority. No user inside or outside Syria can contact another internet user without having to go through that server. This server (computer) stores all the requested information. The Syrian telephone authority is the operator of the internet and also the exclusive provider. It has stated that it will suspend any account that uses encryption programmes.

USA: The Cyberspace Electronic Security Act

The US Justice Department wants the FBI and local police forces to be authorised to secretly enter people's homes to disable security features such as encryption programs on their home computers. Austin Hill, President of Zero-Knowledge – a Canadian privacy company – says:

> 'We've received emails, telephone messages and thousands of sign-ups from people looking to secure their privacy. It's ironic that a Canadian company is being flooded by requests to protect American citizens from their own government. It's disappointing that US consumers must look to other countries for protection from a government they feel is overstepping its investigative authority,' says David Sobel, general counsel for the Electronic Privacy Information Centre (EPIC) in Washington, DC. 'The United States should be in the forefront of privacy technology, not trying to circumvent it.'

Canada

Canada's support for strong privacy solutions contrasts with the US government's stringent controls on encryption and privacy technologies.

United Kingdom

What rights to privacy would you like to be left with in Britain?

2 Big business

In this chapter we will explore:

▶ *the internet harvesters: online databases*
▶ *the danger of registration forms*
▶ *get those kids*
▶ *your browser: the spy within*
▶ *snooping at work*
▶ *giving away your name and number*
▶ *spam, scams and hoaxes*
▶ *case studies*

. . . .

In the process of writing this book, this section – Big Business – began to grow much bigger than the other sections in Part One. It became obvious where the main threat to privacy lies – business greed. There are many ways in which your privacy is threatened by businesses, even if they are legitimate. The most important single aim of all businesses is to part you from your money. In order to realise that aim, businesses need information about you – as much as they can collect.

Many of them greedily suck every piece of information they can legally obtain from anyone that lets them get away with it. Large companies are gathering personal information about consumers at an alarming rate. If that was not bad enough, once they have the information they share it with other companies either willingly at a price or unwillingly through poor security.

Some companies even design computer components and software specially designed to spy on you and report back to them as you surf the web. Other companies gain access to information by using your children. They use cute cartoon characters to win their trust and gently interrogate them. One of the worst threats is from companies who don't care about good business practice and just bombard you with adverts that are often illegal and designed to con you. The amount of information held about you in online databases may astonish you: your previous addresses and employers, your convictions and court judgements, your national insurance number, your shareholdings, your ex-directory phone number, your credit limits and payment histories, and even your bank balance. Aggressive businesses will do almost anything to gain background on people who might send them money.

Many companies are using the internet to exploit people – from simple data collection to downright cons. Most web sites post some form of privacy policy to state how they will use your personal information. But what does this really amount to? Privacy in relation to the internet is a complex and ambiguous matter, and not understood by most consumers. In fact, there is little agreement about what 'online privacy' actually means. Consumers have little idea of what privacy and security are; they are careful of something obvious like credit card details but all kinds of other personal information seeps out over time. The internet can be invasive in the extreme, and allows all kinds of strange individuals and organisations to penetrate into our home.

The internet harvesters: online databases

Information is a commodity that is almost as valuable as money; it is power. Information is the honey that attracts crowds of people to visit a web site. Amongst the most popular sites are search engines that constantly collect and organise information. Search engines are the best sites to find information on any subject on the internet. What happens, though, when the information collected includes data about *you*?

Deja
http://www.deja.com
Deja, for example, collects almost every message posted on Usenet and files it away for years. The messages are stored in a public database that anyone can search by keyword or phrase. The posts on Usenet may be public, but Deja.com, and similar services, enables anyone to build a detailed picture about you and your online habits. Information about you and millions of other people is freely available and easy to find. That information is used to attract people, and the people will then attract advertisers. The more people visit a site, the more the site can charge advertisers.

Companies like Deja will sell the information directly to advertisers in the form of email addresses and other information. The information you let slip in Usenet discussions will end up in dozens of private databases. The more information someone has about you, the more easily they will be able to manipulate your actions and thinking.

Fig. 8. Dejanews maintains a huge and ever-growing database of Usenet posts. Every message you post to a newsgroup will be archived here for public viewing. It will remain there for years to come.

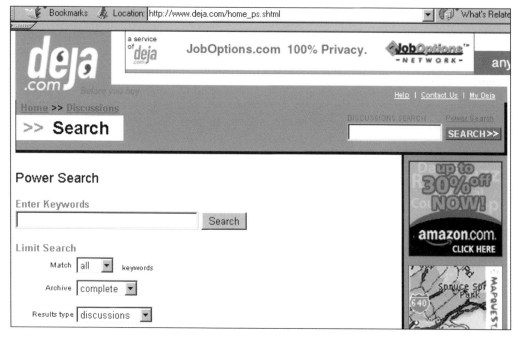

Even if you post messages anonymously, your privacy may be compromised. In America, there is a new legal trend towards violations of privacy going unopposed. Under their terms of service, many American forum operators and ISPs promise not to divulge users' personal information unless requested by a subpoena or court order. However, they do not promise to let you know when a subpoena has been served. So your identity may be disclosed without you knowing. Since subpoenas in civil lawsuits typically don't need the approval of a judge, anyone can file a false lawsuit just to reveal a user's identity. You can, of course, fight the subpoena and preserve your anonymity, but if you don't know about the subpoena in the first place you can't challenge it.

There is nothing new about companies collecting information about you. Supermarkets have been doing it for years by using so-called 'loyalty' cards. Sure, a part of the reason for loyalty cards is to lure customers back to the same store, but a more important reason is to compile information about your buying habits so that the store can target their products more effectively: to make you spend more money. A woman received a letter from the supermarket reminding her that it was time she bought more tampons – she cancelled her loyalty card soon after.

Imagine a supermarket that offers free internet access to its customers – the amount of information that the supermarket already has on you can be used to target online adverts while collecting further information and adding it to your profile. Is this information sold and passed on to other companies without your knowledge? Of course it is.

As another example, when you register a computer or software package online, the chances are you will soon receive junk mail from other companies because the information on your registration form was sold on. Lots of companies are realising that by offering free internet access they can combine all the information gained from your internet activities with the information they already have and with that in databases from other companies. And remember, that information includes:

1. detailed logs of the time you spend online
2. addresses and other details of all the web sites you visit
3. copies of all the emails (and attached files) you send and receive
4. copies of messages and pictures you look at in newsgroups
5. your passwords and user names
6. lists of all the key words you type into search engines

… to name a few.

▶ *Cookies* are small text files which web sites write to your hard disk, probably without your knowledge or permission. Cookies store information about you such as your preferences, your user ID, your password, a list of ads you have seen, your name, etc. Cookies can only be used by the sites which put them there in the first place, but the information collected is often shared between commercial web

Address 🔃 http://www.doubleclick.com/privacy_policy/

DoubleClick
www.doubleclick.net
‹HOME

Case #119: **KRAFT**

"My ad has the holiday blues."

SELECT A CATEGORY | PRIVACY POLICY | SITE MAP | CONTACT US | SEARCH

▶ ADVERTISERS
▶ PUBLISHERS
▶ COMPANY INFO
▼ PRIVACY POLICY
  ⦁ Privacy & Opt Out
▶ LEARNING CENTER
▪ CLIENT LOGIN
SELECT A DOUBLECLICK COUNTRY
Australia ▾
GO

DoubleClick Privacy Statement

Internet user privacy is of paramount importance to DoubleClick, our advertisers and our Web publishers. The success of our business depends upon our ability to maintain the trust of our users. Below is information regarding DoubleClick's commitment to protect the privacy of users and to ensure the integrity of the Internet.

Information Collected in Ad Delivery

In the course of delivering an ad to you, DoubleClick does not collect any personally-identifiable information about you, such as your name, address, phone number or email address. DoubleClick does, however, collect non-personally identifiable information about you, such as the server your computer is logged onto, your browser type (for example, Netscape or Internet Explorer), and whether you responded to the ad

Fig. 9. Doubleclick.com is a top internet marketing company. It makes aggressive use of cookies and bugs to track the activities of millions of people including you as they surf the internet.

sites, and sold on, so that a larger profile of your personal habits can be built up.

Companies like DoubleClick, MatchLogic and AdForce use cookies (see page 36) to tag you with a unique ID number and build a detailed profile based on your online activities. These companies serve dozens of other companies with targeted advertising in the form of banner adverts. Whenever you visit a site that uses one of the banners, the server looks for your ID number, and subsequently analyses and modifies your browsing patterns and other information about you and then shows you an advert that matches your profile. These services even track you when visiting different web sites. For example, if you are browsing Yahoo! then move to the *New York Times* site, the chances are that you will be tracked throughout by several different advertisers.

A result of this tracking is that advertising companies can compile detailed histories of users. For example, DoubleClick, the largest online advertising agency, has a network of more than 9,000 sites. It can build a detailed 'clickstream' history showing exactly which of those sites you visit and when. Even the British or American governments might struggle to main this enormous scale of surveillance.

The danger of registration forms

You will often go to a site expecting lots of useful information, only to be refused entry until you fill in a registration form full of personal questions. Some questionnaires have just a few simple questions, for example asking your name and how you heard about the site. Others

30

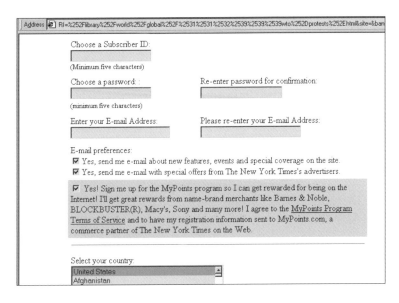

Fig. 10. The *New York Times* online registration form. This is an example of the forms that companies use to try and harvest detailed information about your internet habits.

demand answers to a comprehensive list of questions that the FBI would be proud of. Many of the registration forms force you to provide details such as name, sex, age, date of birth, marital status, telephone number, address, type of computer, income, interests, children's names, and so on before you can proceed. The site will refuse to 'let you in' unless you provide the information.

This kind of pushy and intrusive behaviour – used by many well-known companies – is an irritating and unacceptable violation of privacy. It would be almost like the doorman of a restaurant not letting you past until you have handed over your wallet, organiser and the keys to your house. You would be well advised to walk away.

Registration forms should always have an option to allow you to deny permission for the web site to share the information with other companies. The option is usually in small print, and set up so that it grants permission by default. If you opt not to let the company share your information, they usually 'promise' to keep your details 'confidential' but once they are in the database, it only takes a small policy change, a company takeover, a bankruptcy, or a lapse in security for them to fall into other hands. Once one of the huge marketing companies gets a hold of the information, it will be almost impossible preventing the spread to other companies.

Printed magazines routinely sell their subscribers' personal details to advertising companies. Online companies are following suit. If you fill in registration forms, expect the worst unless you follow some precautions. Before filling in registration details ask yourself some questions:

1. Can you really trust the site not to sell your information?
2. Can you choose not to accept junk mail?
3. Can you easily enter false information into the form?

If the answer is no to any of the above, then go to another site or be prepared to receive an increasing flood of junk mail both by email and snail mail.

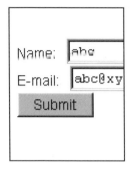

Giving false details
Approximately a third of all people on the internet put in false information when filling out online registration forms. Many simply enter random keys in the various fields, just to get it over with, and onto the site itself. There is a small risk of your access to the site being blocked if you are 'found out' but it will only need another trip to the registration site to get back in. To find out how to minimise the amount of information that you leak onto the internet, see page 71.

Get those kids

When we think of the risks to children, we imagine pornography and violence. Certainly those threats are there, but there is a more insidious threat from businesses that target children in their marketing campaigns.

Many of the colourful sites for children are really fronts for aggressive corporations. The sites offer incentives of prizes and lots of fun and games, but only after the child has filled out a long questionnaire, which asks for personal information about themselves and sometimes their parents.

Some advertisers exploit children's weaknesses in order to ram a brand name down the child's throat. Nancy Shalek, president of the Shalek Agency, admitted to the *Los Angeles Times*:

'Advertising at its best is making people feel that, without their product, you're a loser. Kids are very sensitive to that. If you tell them to buy something, they are resistant. But if you tell them that they'll be a dork if they don't, you've got their attention. You open up emotional vulnerabilities and it's very easy to do with kids because they're the most emotionally vulnerable.'

Some advertisers openly admit that their aim is to control children's minds. Mike Searles, former president of Kids-R-Us, the large children's clothing store, said that 'If you own this child at an early age, you can own this child for years to come.'

An example of a site that collects a large amount of information is KidsCom. It insists on children registering before they can 'join in the fun'. Registration involves answering all the normal questions such as name, sex, date of birth, and many other more personal questions such as: how many people are there living in the same house, what your interests are, what is your favourite television program, and what do you want to be when older. The site revolves around a points system. By playing and winning certain games and quizzes, the child can earn points. When enough points have been won, the child can redeem them for goods.

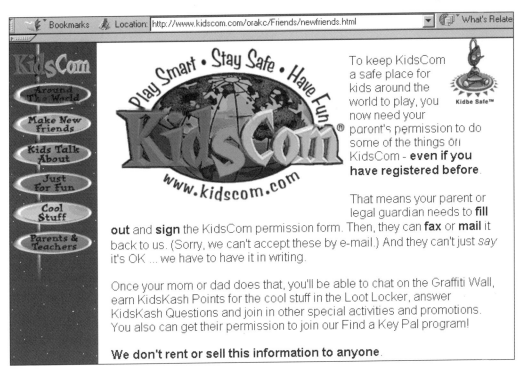

To keep KidsCom a safe place for kids around the world to play, you now need your parent's permission to do some of the things on KidsCom - **even if you have registered before**.

That means your parent or legal guardian needs to **fill out** and **sign** the KidsCom permission form. Then, they can **fax** or **mail** it back to us. (Sorry, we can't accept these by e-mail.) And they can't just *say* it's OK ... we have to have it in writing.

Once your mom or dad does that, you'll be able to chat on the Graffiti Wall, earn KidsKash Points for the cool stuff in the Loot Locker, answer KidsKash Questions and join in other special activities and promotions. You also can get their permission to join our Find a Key Pal program!

We don't rent or sell this information to anyone.

An organisation called the Centre for Media Education (CME) is leading the campaign against online exploitation of children for marketing purposes. CME has listed the various forms of bad practice that many firms are resorting to. These include:

1. Monitoring the online activities of children in order to collect personal information.
2. Using competitions and games to extract personal information from children.
3. Using the information to present ads personalised to the individual child.
4. Immersing the child in an environment – game, fantasy world – made up of branded images and characters.

The online experience of the children is often managed so that they are unaware of the advertising information which surrounds them and which constantly tries to influence their buying decisions.

The attitude of many big companies which target children is well known to be concerned only with using them as sources of profit. McDonalds' operations manual, for example, reveals the truth with this instruction to its employees: 'Ronald loves McDonald's and McDonald's food. And so do children, because they love Ronald. Remember that children exert a phenomenal influence when it comes to restaurant selection. This means that you should do everything you can to appeal to children's love for Ronald and McDonald's.'[1]

Fig. 11. Kidscom attracts children with its bright colours and cartoon characters and lets the children join in the fun but only after filling in a long registration form with invasive personal questions.

1. Source: http://www.mcspotlight.org/trial/news/tnews.html#manual

The CME reports that alcohol and tobacco companies – faced with strict regulation in other media – are now trying to hook children on the web. They are mixing in their advertising propaganda with games, stories, chat areas, and even career advice. To see how you can protect your children while they are on the internet, see page 112.

Your browser: the spy within

You may think that your web browser is your tool to enable you to enjoy exploring the internet. But in reality, it is spying on you. As you browse the web, it busily collects information about you and allows its real master – big business – to collect other information about you. The browser can also be used maliciously to sabotage and damage your computer, your reputation, and your wallet.

▶ *Browser* – A computer program that allows you to retrieve and view web sites. Internet Explorer, Netscape Navigator, and Opera are common browsers.

Fig. 12. Internet Explorer copies to your hard disk all the web pages you visit, in order to speed up browsing. The files in this cache ('Temporary Internet Files') are easily visible to any casual snooper who may get hold of your computer, now or at any time in the future.

The cache

Among the information that your browser collects is the address and content of web pages that you have most recently visited. This includes the text, graphics and sound files on those pages. All this is stored in a cache on your hard drive. The cache provides a detailed record of your surfing activities to whoever else uses your computer, if they know where to look. The next user could be your child, spouse, boss, colleague, friend, computer repairman, tax inspector, VAT inspector or other official investigator. The same applies to the browser's list of recently visited sites and the favourites or bookmarks. These features were designed to let surfers view sites offline and to make their surfing experience faster, but if others want to find out what you have been up to, they can easily do so.

Logs

Web-browsers like Internet Explorer and Netscape are actually designed to give certain information away without telling you. When you look at a web site, the chance is that your browser is providing certain information about you, such as who you are and what parts of the site you visit. The site then collects this information in a log. These logs are often made available to anybody who knows how to view them. Here is an example of part of a log:

```
userap39.uk.uudial.com - - [10/Mar/1999:13:44:06 +0000] "GET
/default.htm HTTP/1.0" 200 8610
userap39.uk.uudial.com - - [10/Mar/1999:13:44:07 +0000] "GET
/ HTTP/1.0" 200 -
userap39.uk.uudial.com - - [10/Mar/1999:13:44:07 +0000] "GET
/.themes/ukwriter/punched%20paper2.gif HTTP/1.0" 200 1145
userap39.uk.uudial.com - - [10/Mar/1999:13:44:08 +0000] "GET
/.themes/ukwriter/modhorsa.gif HTTP/1.0" 200 134
userap39.uk.uudial.com - - [10/Mar/1999:13:44:08 +0000] "GET
/.themes/ukwriter/modbul1a.gif HTTP/1.0" 200 84
userap39.uk.uudial.com - - [10/Mar/1999:13:44:09 +0000] "GET
/cgi/nph-count?width=5&link=/www.ukwriters.com/default.htm
HTTP/1.0" 200 -
userap39.uk.uudial.com - - [10/Mar/1999:13:44:09 +0000] "GET
/images/logo.gif HTTP/1.0" 206 1881
```

The internet address 'userap39.uk.uudial.com' may not be immediately identifiable, but by combining logs with other methods of information collection, it can be simplicity itself.

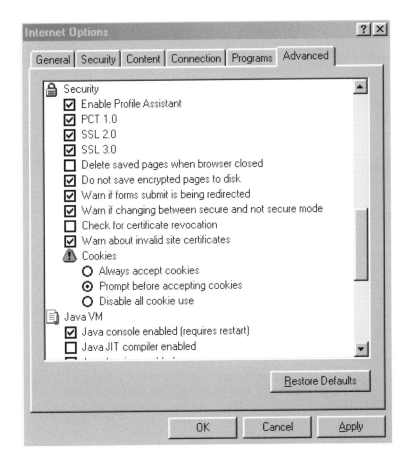

Fig. 13. Adjusting the cookie settings in Internet Explorer. Cookies can give companies more information about you than you think. These little text files act as mini-spies on your hard disk. You can 'disable all cookie use'.

Cookies

Imagine you walk into a shop and, unknown to you, a small transmitter is attached to your back. As you walk around the shop, the transmitter keeps track of your movements, which products you have looked at, how long you looked and what, if anything, you bought. The transmitter knows your name, address and much more.

The next time you visit the store, everything is eerily arranged the way you like it. You later find that other shops start to welcome you by name and make you aware of certain products that you 'may find interesting'. You may by this time start to realise that something strange is happening: that the shops are sharing information about you. You may even have worked out that it is the bug that allows the shops to share information about you and that they each add their own observations to your growing dossier. Can you imagine the scandal and uproar that would follow if high street shops really did this?

Fig. 14. If you use Internet Explorer, all arriving cookies are stored in the Windows Cookies folder. By opening this folder you can view, delete, or alter them, just like any other text files.

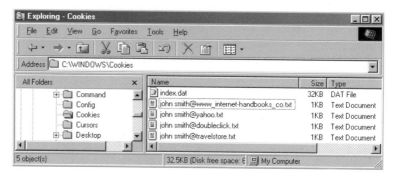

High street shops may not do this kind of thing yet but sites on the web are doing it already with bugs called cookies. Instead of attaching the bugs to your coat, they put it on your computer hard drive where it stays hidden and is made available to any site that has access to it. Many of the sites that place these bugs are part of a network of collaborating sites, sometimes thousands of them, that pool information about your 'movements' and activities on the web.

Sites store cookies on the hard drive of your computer because it is the simplest way to track your activities at the site without alerting you that you are being tracked. Here is an example of the contents of a cookie from a company called DoubleClick:

	Id
Your unique ID number	bf67cd52
The domain that can retrieve the information	DoubleClick.net/
	0
Other information	1468938752
	31583413
	3643917984
	29305321
	*

Cookies were originally intended to make browsing an easier and more enjoyable experience and in many cases they do just that. They allow a great deal of customisation in the way you see a web page. Yahoo! for instance allows you to customise your view of their page so that it includes specific information and news that you find interests you.

Fig. 15. My Yahoo! uses cookies to customise its web site to your preferences, so at least the 'spy' is doing something to help you. This is how cookies should be used.

Say you wanted sports news only; you could select what kind of news you want to see and that information is stored in a cookie. The next time you go to the Yahoo! site, it looks at the information in the cookie and shows you the type of information that you previously selected and then tailors the site to your interests.

Other sites use cookies to store your user name and password to save you having to typing them in each time you visit. In many cases cookies can make browsing easier and friendlier. The possibilities to make browsing more enjoyable are almost endless, whenever personal preferences or other data needs to be saved it can be saved as a cookie. The downside is that they also allow you to be tracked and your movements to be recorded by using a unique identifying number. Unfortunately, many sites use cookies for tracking purposes without giving you anything useful in return.

▶ *Why are cookies stored on my computer and not on the web site's?* – For the same reason that you are given a supermarket loyalty card with its own unique number. Imagine how difficult it would be for the staff in a supermarket to remember the names of all their customers. Similarly, a company like Amazon or Yahoo! would have to remember preferences for the millions of people who visit them. If the preferences had to be stored on their own server, it would take up a huge amount of disk space. A much better way is to store just a little information in the form of cookies on a user's own computer.

Whether you see cookies as useful   nvasion of privacy depends on your viewpoint and how much yo.   ue your privacy. It is a balance

Big business . . . .

Fig. 16. The Netscape browser allows you to see who is trying to place cookies onto your computer. You can use Edit, Preferences, to accept or disable them, or to warn you each time one arrives.

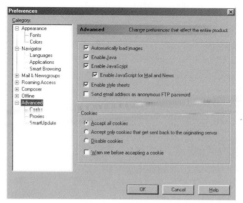

between convenience and privacy; if you can do without the ability to customise how you see web sites and you don't mind occasionally typing in your password then 'disable cookies' in your web-browser (see page 80).

Cookies can't damage your computer directly, or be used to get anything from your computer, but if you give a site information by (e.g. by typing it into a form) it will be able to store it in a cookie and share it with others in the same network. A cookie is only a holder for information, but once cookies are cross-referenced with logs or other data sources, then the dossier on you can become alarmingly comprehensive.

Another thing to be aware of is that most of the search engines will put cookies on your hard drive, and could save your search keywords in a cookie. Be careful what you search for; you might get more than you bargained for.

Handle with care: scripts, Java applets and ActiveX
Modern browsers are far more than just document viewers, they can also allow web pages to perform complicated tasks on the web, or even on your own computer. Embedded in some web pages are programs. When you view one of these pages, your browser downloads the programs along with the rest of the contents. Once one of these programs is on your computer, your browser interprets the instructions and carries them out.

Many of these programs are not harmful at all. On the contrary, they are extremely useful. But in the hands of someone with a little knowledge, a lot of damage can be caused such as deleting files or revealing private information.

▶ *Program* – A series of coded instructions that will automatically control a computer in carrying out a specific task. Java, JavaScript VBScript, and ActiveX are languages that programs are written in.

There are three main types of program: scripts, applets and controls.

Scripts
A script is a set of commands written into the HTML tags of a web page. Script languages such as JavaScript and VBScript are designed for non-programmers to use, rather like using macros in a word processor. Scripts are hidden from view, but are executed when you open a page or click a link containing script instructions. The main reason why scripts are common is that web designers can copy scripts which perform common tasks and use them in their own pages without having to be

a programming wizard.

▶ *HTML* – the language that a web page is usually written in (hyper text mark-up language)

JavaScript can make a site more dynamic and interactive. For example, graphical effects like links that change colour or pictures that change when you pass the mouse over them. Scripts are also used to perform some more complicated tasks such as games like hangman or noughts and crosses and calculations of mortgages etc.

JavaScript was a great idea, but unfortunately it was not tested properly and contains many weaknesses that can be exploited. Some of the first weaknesses in JavaScript were discovered by a 15-year-old who found them by accident as he was 'playing around'. Since then, many more bugs have been discovered. In the wrong hands, JavaScript can perform malicious tasks such as capturing your username and password.

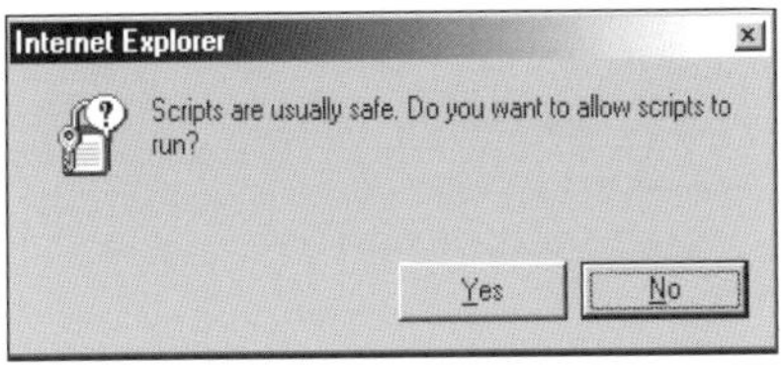

In October 1999, for example, Microsoft announced that Internet Explorer 5 could allow malicious scripts on web sites to gain access to a visitor's computer. The attack uses Explorer's download behaviour feature, which is intended to allow web page authors to download files for use with some scripts. This means that the files on your computer, and your network if you have one, are vulnerable. Microsoft have now made a fix available, see page 88.

Fig. 17. Both Internet Explorer and Netscape can warn you before a script starts to run, but you will need to change the settings first. However, the constant warnings being flashed up will soon get on your nerves better to disable cookies completely.

VBScript is similar to JavaScript but is not as common and, for this reason, there are fewer malicious scripts around.

Java applets

Whereas the instructions of JavaScript are contained in the web page, those of Java are in separate files called applets. Java is a much more complicated, and powerful, language. It can perform correspondingly more complicated and spectacular tasks.

An applet is a small computer program that runs on your computer. An example of an applet could be a financial calculator that keeps track of the rate of exchange of various currencies in real time. The application could refer to the web site for up to the minute rates and let you calculate accordingly. Another applet could be a drawing program for a child.

▶ *Applet* – an application programmed in Java that is designed to run mainly on web browsers. Usually applets are useful or at least harmless. Sometimes, however, they can cause serious security problems.

When your browser receives a Java applet, it executes the program one instruction at a time and, in theory, the browser monitors the execution so that nothing harmful is done to your computer.

Java was developed by Sun Microsystems for professional programmers. It is similar to other powerful programming languages, but with the ability to create destructive programs taken away – or so it was claimed. A Java program should not be able to inspect or change files on your computer or bypass file protection mechanisms.

The theory is that Java runs on a virtual computer in your real computer's memory and can do no damage outside of that virtual computer. The truth, however, is that your computer is still vulnerable. There have been many cases of Java causing breaches of security; some as bad as causing computers to reboot and thus lose all unsaved data. But not even Java is the biggest threat to security: ActiveX is the real villain.

ActiveX

Microsoft's answer to Java and JavaScript was ActiveX. ActiveX is a wonderful tool when it is working as it should. Sites designed with ActiveX components often have stunning effects and are easy to use. The same tools, however, can be used maliciously to devastating effect.

Fig. 18. Even after disabling ActiveX controls in Internet Explorer, you will still receive repeated and annoying warnings when you visit sites that use ActiveX controls. The only option is to use another browser such as Netscape.

ActiveX is not a programming language, nor does it use the virtual machine technique of Java. It involves small programs that have complete access to your computer. An ActiveX component could easily be written, for example, to scan your computer for all documents. It could then send them to your local con man, criminal organisation, large corporation, police, tax office or other state agency. A malicious programmer could easily install a computer virus on a system, turn off all the security features, read personal files, upload them secretly to a remote web site, delete document files from your hard drive, and remove system files so that your system will no longer start.[3]

▶ *Virus* - a small program that can reproduce itself and cause damage to equipment and data stored on computer systems. All computer viruses are man-made and even a simple virus can cause irreparable damage.

Don't assume you can safeguard yourself by not downloading any ActiveX controls – some computers have many ActiveX controls preinstalled. Some of them are dangerous and can be easily misused on a web page to gain access to the computer and run other programs. Script instructions can be embedded in an email message which will launch programs and read and write to the Windows registry, which controls many of the functions of Windows-based computers.

3. Source: *Risks Digest 20.50* posted on the usenet Risks newsgroup: comp.risks

One security expert managed to construct a test email message containing a few lines of JavaScript. The script indirectly downloads a Windows executable file,

installs it on the hard drive then executes it. For his test he downloaded and ran the Windows calculator program but the same method could be used to run a virus or any other harmful program. It was as easy as pie: Outlook Express fetched the email message and ran the script automatically as soon as the message was read.

The same expert also found another pre-installed ActiveX control (specific to Hewlett Packard computers) on his computer that could give out information such as name, address, and phone number to a web site. The control was intended to simplify registration for owners of Hewlett Packard machines but could potentially be used by other, less trustworthy, organisations and individuals.

▶ *Tip* – A site that will allow you to test which potentially unsafe ActiveX controls are installed on your system is: http://www.tiac.-net/users/smiths/acctroj/axcheck.htm

Safe or not?

When your browser downloads an ActiveX control, it checks whether it is marked 'safe for scripting' or whether it is signed. What does that mean? Well, clearly, people are not going to trust all controls that can be found on the internet so Microsoft and other companies had to develop a system where controls could be authenticated in some way, preferably by a certificate. The system is called Authenticode.

▶ *Authenticode* – a system where ActiveX controls can be authenticated in some way, usually by a certificate.

In January 1997 members of a group called the Chaos Computer Club showed how an ActiveX program could take control of a PC and transfer funds from an online bank account without the user's knowledge. Microsoft responded to the announcement by saying that their technology known as Authenticode could prevent such malicious ActiveX controls from being downloaded. It said that (a) it would identify the author of the ActiveX controls, and (b) it would determine that the control hadn't been tampered with.

When a software company wants to release an ActiveX control, it obtains a digital certificate from a recognised authentication company VeriSign – which provides them with a verified and encrypted certificate. If a control has no certificate, your browser will give you a warning message.

If it has a certificate, any web page can activate the control without having to request your permission or give you notification. The problem is that, at one time, it was possible to falsely obtain a certificate from

Fig. 20. The Chaos Computer Club is a respected organisation. It aims to create greater public awareness on issues like security and privacy, based on a more informed and open viewpoint than is usually available.

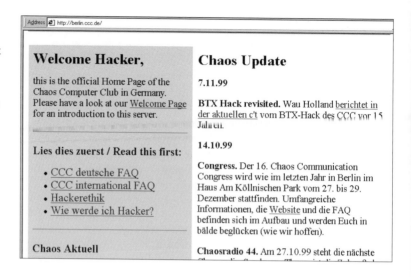

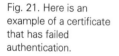

VeriSign. There was no validation and no enforceable rules. A certificate – even a valid one – does not say that the control is safe. It only says who it comes from.

So it's not hard to imagine some nasty person putting an even nastier control on a web site. The only thing then standing between the user and disaster is Microsoft's requirement that controls be signed. Most users confronted by an official-looking certificate will just click OK, no matter who has signed it. Hopefully by the time you read this book, Microsoft will have solved the problem.

Fig. 21. Here is an example of a certificate that has failed authentication.

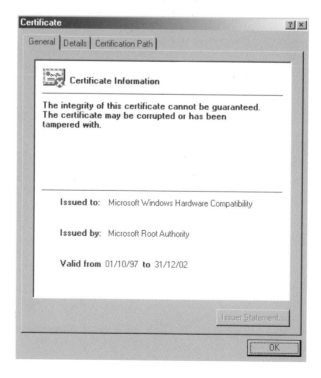

Snooping at work

Many organisations in the private and pubic sectors track their employees as they use the internet. Increasing use of these connections for non-company business such as travel bookings, or viewing sports sites and pornography, is driving companies to monitor their employees' internet usage and take action when the internet is not used for business. There are many examples of people becoming unstuck when their email messages fell into the wrong hands. To be fair, employers have every right to monitor your internet use. After all, they are paying for your time at work, and could be sued if you commit an indiscretion such as making a comment about a competing company on the internet.

Deleting an email message is no protection, nor is clearing your browser's cache and history list. You could throw your computer out of the window and there would *still* be a record of your internet activities elsewhere on the network. Messages and other files are routinely stored and backed up in a central location.

▶ *Deleting files* – Even if your computer is not on a network, 'deleting' a file is not what it seems. 'Delete' often means no more than marking as free the space formerly occupied by that file. The file information remains on the hard disk until overwritten by another file (which could be a very long time). A person with quite basic computer knowledge could easily 'undelete' (restore) and view that 'deleted' file.

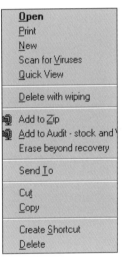

It is understandable if an employer monitors your email traffic and web activities, but it may not be just your employer who is snooping on you. Office rivalry can become fierce, and if a competitive colleague finds out your password the temptation for them to snoop on your work or 'put the boot in' can become irresistible. Once a person logs on with your username and password, they can access all of your email messages from any computer on the network – so keep your password close to your chest and change it from time to time (see page 72).

Giving away your name and number

Pentium III serial numbers: what you should know

The FBI is keen to encourage new technical means to identify internet users, and to limit people's freedom to communicate anonymously. Privacy activists warn that Intel's Pentium III computers may well be the FBI's wish come true.

All Pentium III computers have a unique electronic identification number built into the circuitry. This number is made available to web sites so they can identify and possibly track you as you move from site to site throughout cyber space. With some computer knowledge you can deactivate the feature. However, history shows that companies often try to coerce people into leaving it active.

These unique serial numbers identify the processor, and by association, your computer – and you. The in-built IDs will inevitably be used to

Big business ....

Fig. 22. On its web site, the leading computer chip manufacturer Intel has tried to play down the privacy issues surrounding the use of Pentium III personal serial numbers. Instead, it emphasises the benefits of the serial number to software developers.

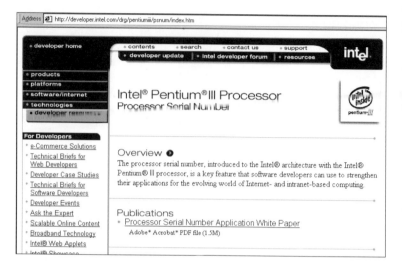

link you with your online purchases and to provide a method for gathering more information about your web-browsing habits. As Intel's web page states: 'Some of the most popular internet communities on the web will use the Pentium III processor as a virtual access card'. This has its good sides but can also be abused by marketing companies and others to further increase their dossier on you.

Intel admits that the serial number can be used by web sites to identify you when conducting ecommerce, or when accessing member-only areas. The serial number when used in combination with other data – such as an electronic fingerscan or PIN could also be used to build databases of user habits, trace email, and many other things.

Intel says that the processor serial number will not be made public over the internet, and so users need not worry. But the number may well be available to any site that asks for it and without telling you that it has done so. When a web site wishes to access the encoded number (according to Intel), it must first send an applet to the user's system, read the serial number, and then report it back to the web site. Web browsers can be set to provide a notification when such applets are trying to run on your system, but this feature is usually turned off by default. Most inexperienced users will never realise that their number is being read.

If Intel manages to establish this as a standard, some prominent web sites will begin to refuse entry unless your ID is turned on. And, as online purchases steadily increase, sites are going to demand some method to identify purchasers so that you can be traced if there is any problem, or to assess you for new internet taxes. It is also likely that software packages will require users to enable the ID before the software works. The serial number being available is not the problem. That it will be given out without your permission – and without your knowing – *is* a big problem.

Some people say that the serial number will probably replace credit card details as the prime target of amateur hackers and crackers. Patches and programs will show up at hacker web sites, enabling anyone to fake the serial number in order to impersonate others, or maintain their privacy. In cases where several people share a computer, serious problems could also arise if they accidentally or maliciously impersonated you.

▶ *Example* – Suppose that your employer chooses to lobby the government for longer working hours. And suppose that you are opposed to the proposal, and make your feelings clear in a Usenet newsgroup, using your internet account at home. Your employer might buy a list of all Pentium serial numbers that had been used to write critical posts, and then cross-reference that list with one of computers sold through the company discount program. They would then find out that you had opposed company policy, outside your place of work. Your name and address may even be directly available on some online directory service that uses the ID numbers.

Remember that the number will be available at every link in the chain, and the *only* person whom it will not benefit is *you*. It will be used for marketing, billing, priority, industrial security, etc. If it's available, it will be used to further the cause of big business.

What if an insurance company scanned the medical newsgroups and records all of the serial numbers of those people with serious medical complaints? If you had ever used such a group, or if someone had once forged your number, you could find that you are asked to pay a high premium for medical insurance or even be refused – without ever knowing why.

Finding out more about the Pentium III problem
The PIII serial number is a key that makes it practical to carry out personal data collection on a massive and global scale. Read more at: http://www.heise.de/ct/english/99/05/news1/

▶ *Tip* – If you are buying or upgrading a home computer, ask the supplier whether or not it contains a Pentium III chip, and whether the personal identification number is switched on or off. Learn how to switch it on or off yourself.

Microsoft Office GUID: how it affects you
In 1999, Microsoft Corporation was confronted with the fact that documents created by its Word and Excel programs had unique numbers embedded in them that could potentially identify the author's computer. It was later discovered that the number, a Globally Unique Identifier (GUID), was also being transmitted to Microsoft by the Windows 98 registration wizard, which allows customers to register for support and updates.

At about the same time, it was alleged that Microsoft was building a database of personal information in the form of digital fingerprints that were able to match documents to particular computers. A response was published on Microsoft's web site: Yusuf Mehdi, director of Windows Marketing, said that Microsoft was taking the following steps to address the privacy issues raised by the GUID.

1. Modify the Windows 98 Registration Wizard in an update of the operating system. The modified wizard would not automatically send a GUID unless the user chose to allow it to.

2. Provide a software tool that would allow users to delete registration information from the Windows registry.

3. Investigate whether any hardware ID information is stored on Microsoft databases and purge where found.

Fig. 23. Microsoft makes a statement about the GUID numbers that permeate its Windows programs.

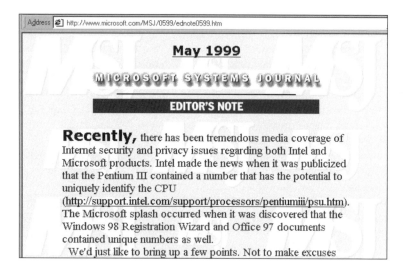

Address http://www.microsoft.com/MSJ/0599/ednote0599.htm

May 1999

MICROSOFT SYSTEMS JOURNAL

EDITOR'S NOTE

Recently, there has been tremendous media coverage of Internet security and privacy issues regarding both Intel and Microsoft products. Intel made the news when it was publicized that the Pentium III contained a number that has the potential to uniquely identify the CPU (http://support.intel.com/support/processors/pentiumiii/psu.htm). The Microsoft splash occurred when it was discovered that the Windows 98 Registration Wizard and Office 97 documents contained unique numbers as well.
We'd just like to bring up a few points. Not to make excuses

In fact, GUIDs – originally designed to make it easier for programs to communicate with one another – are embedded in almost every program that runs in Microsoft Windows, so avoiding the use of GUIDs may be impossible.

For good or for bad, unique identification numbers seem to be an inevitable part of the future. The general lack of opposition to the Pentium III numbers suggests that the general public don't care (or don't realise) what the consequences could be. Hopefully, as mass information harvesting becomes more common, legislation in different countries will also force companies to be accountable to the public and make it clear, as in the UK Data Protection Act or better, how the information is being used.

Internet serial numbers

Messages and other types of communications that fly around the internet all have a source and a destination. All need an address if they are to be delivered to that destination. The address of each packet of information is included as part of the packet, just like a parcel sent by normal mail. But there is a new internet addressing system being developed, called IPv6.

This may also include some kind of unique serial number similar to the Pentium III computers. The new system could attach a unique serial number from each personal computer to every parcel of data. Privacy campaigners fear the idea could lead to senders' identities being easily traceable – good if you are tracing money laundering transactions, but bad if used by big business for money making, or by a heavy-handed government for tracking private individuals for one reason or another.

These addresses, planted within emails and all other information flowing across the internet, must be as unique as telephone numbers, to distinguish each computer on the global network and to guide the billions of bits and bytes flowing among them.

'I'm just winding the tape forward five years, to when we all say, "Oh, my God!" said Richard Smith, a US security expert who was among the first to question the new plan. Marc Rotenberg of Electronic Privacy Information Centre said: 'There's no doubt there are serious privacy concerns.'

It is obvious that commercial internet sites, which already record your IP addresses in their logs, could correlate these embedded serial numbers against a person's name, address and other personal details such as skin colour, political preference, sexual orientation, medical history, religious affiliation and shoe size.

▶ *IP address* – the address of a computer or device on the internet.

The new system may not become widely used for some years yet. If it does gain wide acceptance, it will ultimately affect every internet user.

Spam, scams and hoaxes

Spam, and unsolicited commercial email (UCE), are terms that refer to junk mail. This can be either sent to you personally by email, or posted across lots – sometimes hundreds – of newsgroups. The term 'spam' was borrowed from a *Monty Python* sketch. It has come to refer to the

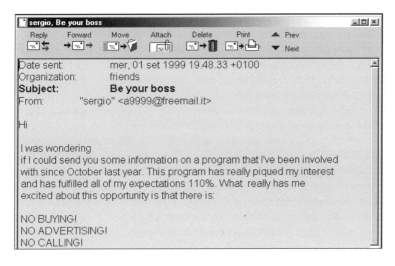

Fig. 24. Here is an example of junk email. The tell-tale signs of a con include usually include repeated exclamation marks, the word FREE, and the mention of a lot of easy money.

practice of sending hundreds or thousands of unwanted messages to Usenet or individuals. The email version of spam usually has a title that gives it away such as '!!!!How I made five thousand pounds in a single day!!!!' All spam is unwanted and a lot of it is illegal in many countries.

If you are new to the internet, the junk mailers may not have noticed you yet and your mailbox will be fairly quiet. But, rest assured, once you have shown your head, they will see you as fair game. The first few shots usually come after you have posted your first Usenet message. You feel elated at having spoken your piece to the world and are expecting some congratulatory replies and what do you find instead? A message promising you the secret to making a million pounds in a year 'as soon as you send £5 to the sender of the junk message'. What a come down.

Spam on Usenet usually refers to the sending of identical or similar messages to many different Usenet groups at the same time. Spam and UCE are both similar in that neither is requested or relevant like the normal junk mail we receive through our letterboxes. The main difference between postal junk mail and internet junk mail is that the leaflets we get through the door do not cost you anything but internet junk mail adds to your phone bill because you have to download it before you can tell it is junk.

For example, with normal marketing practice, a company wanting to reach a wider audience could print a catalogue and have them delivered to everyone in the surrounding area. The company would bear the cost of printing and delivery. You contribute nothing apart from a little space in your rubbish bin, you are not charged each time you receive one. The cost of normal junk-mail campaigns involves a large financial outlay by the mailer. That outlay acts as a restraint, ensuring that the quantity of junk mail is limited.

On the other hand, the cost of an email advertising campaign is negligible for the advertising company. There are no printing costs – text is generated and distributed electronically, and there are no delivery costs. Internet junk mail is delivered over the internet. The financial restraints that keep the normal junk mailers under control are just not there for the spammer.

You pay to receive junk
Many internet users, particularly those who use premier online services such as AOL and CompuServe, are charged for each email message they receive. That is, the users are paying to receive advertisements along with genuine email messages, even though they did not ask for them. The spammers are practically stealing money from you.

Even users who access the internet via ISPs that do not charge per message received are out of pocket. They must pay for the telephone bill which is increased because of the time spent downloading email messages.

After a few months on the internet, the number of junk email messages you receive could, in a bad case, rise into double figures a day. Say you receive 10 a day (some people do) that's 70 a week and over 3,000 each year. Suppose those messages take an average of just ten seconds to download. That will add over eight hours each year to your telephone bill. And today's 10 unwanted messages could become 10,000 as the internet grows in size.

It may be argued that it costs very little for those extra few seconds required to download UCE. But if you were to add up the costs of those extra seconds over your internet lifetime, it could amount to hundreds or thousands of pounds out of your taxed income.

Because of this, UCE is an unacceptable form of advertising and differs from traditional junk mail, which is delivered at the advertiser's expense. UCE is the equivalent of a salesman stuffing his shoe in your door to prevent you closing it then charging you for the privilege.

UCE wastes your time

Most people use email for business or personal use only. It is a medium through which family and business colleagues can contact each other quickly and efficiently. As such, you may set aside a certain amount of time each day to read and respond to your email.

UCE wastes time that could otherwise be spent more profitably or constructively. Instead of communicating with people, you will spend an increasing amount of time wading through the dross in your mailbox identifying and deleting UCE.

One of the main arguments in support of UCE is that people who are uninterested can simply delete the email, with no harm done. Not true – that argument is only used by those who have something to gain by sending out millions of junk email ads. As mentioned above, it takes time and money to download the email and further time to pick out the real messages.

Most advertisers try to disguise their ads so you think it is a message from a friend or colleague. There are no subject headers warning readers that the enclosed email is a marketing ploy. They realise that it is no use

```
Message Source                                          _ □ ×
Received: from post.corpex.com (post.corpex.com [195.153.24
        by yacko.madasafish.com (8.8.8+Sun/8.8.8) with SMTP i
        for <molly@madasafish.com>; Tue, 30 Nov 1999 18:16:00
From: adsl@ms37.url.com.tw
Received: (qmail 2745 invoked by uid 6572); 30 Nov 1999 18:
Delivered-To: bphjkh-admin@ukwriters.com
Received: (qmail 2742 invoked by uid 0); 30 Nov 1999 18:00:
MBOX-Line: From ms37.url.com.tw!adsl Tue Nov 30 18:00:04 19
Received: from m4.is.net.tw([210.62.128.24]) (1638 bytes) b
        via smail with P:smtp/R:bind_hosts/T:smtp-filter
        (sender: <adsl@ms37.url.com.tw>)
        id <m11srZK-003xmPC@mail.corpex.com>
        for <admin@ukwriters.com>; Tue, 30 Nov 1999 18:00:02 -
        (Smail-3.2.0.105 1999-Mar-3 #3 built 1999-Mar-26)
Received: from m2.is.net.tw (c76.h203149190.is.net.tw [203.
        id BAA07506 for <admin@ukwriters.com>; Wed, 1 Dec 199
Message-Id: <199911301757.BAA07506@m4.is.net.tw>
To: <admin@ukwriters.com>
Subject: ³oü$¥¿¬0$A¹Ú´K¥H´Dª°¡aׯë
Date: ¬P´Á¤T, 1 ¤Q¤G¤ë 1999 01:24:23
Content-Type: text
Content-Length: 1091
Status:
```

Fig. 25. This is an example of a full (as against a brief) email header. The important parts that reveal the identity of the real sender are the 'Received' lines. The bottom 'Received' usually identifies the sender's ISP. If it is forged, work your way up through the other 'Received' lines.

simply sending junk email: they need to make sure you actually read the ad. Methods range from vague or non-existent subject headers, to personalised headers that give you the impression that the email message has been sent from a friend or a colleague.

> ▶ *Header* – The header is the part of a message that contains information about the subject of the message, the sender and the route that the message took through the internet.

At the moment, you might only receive a few items of junk each day, which may not take long to deal with. However, if UCE receives widespread acceptance, expect many more than just a few messages a day. There are thousands of marketers dying to send you junk email. If UCE was ever accepted, the amount of junk received would soon far outstrip your legitimate email, if it doesn't already.

Junk clogs up the internet
Spam also costs you money because it can slow the whole internet down. UCE is almost always sent to hundreds, or thousands of people. This adds an unnecessary extra burden to an already limited and strained internet. Whenever you find your connection slow or dead, or as you watch the minutes grow whilst waiting for a file to download, imagine how much faster it might be if there weren't hundreds of thousands of junk messages flooding onto the internet by advertisers after a 'quick buck'. How much less would your telephone bill be after that saved time?

Scams
There are more than 200 million internet users worldwide, and the number is growing very quickly. All are potential targets for con artists who can find and contact victims quickly and cheaply, and disappear without a trace at the least sign of trouble. They can seem very impressive. They often put up a front by using professional-looking web sites and realistic email adverts that look as professional or more so than the well-established companies. Once bitten, internet fraud victims have little chance of redress. The best defence is to apply the precautions described in the second half of this book.

Email is the most common way to spread fraudulent adverts in the form of thousands of UCE messages or Usenet spam. The internet makes it easy for them to collect thousands of email addresses and bombard masses of people with their con. Some people will always fall for it. The simplest way for them to collect email addresses of victims is to use a service such as Deja.com or to use a program to automatically scan web sites and Usenet posts for addresses. The more sophisticated con man may break into the network of a large company or ISP such as America Online and download account names and addresses. They may then use the information themselves or sell it to others. This kind of computer fraud may involve special software (see Trojan horses on page 59) that taps into private information such as social security numbers or credit card accounts.

Most cons use spam but web sites can also serve to pull the wool over our eyes. Cyberspace has become the new frontier for con artists. The medium may be different but the cons are not. Fraudulent dealers use email and web sites to promote familiar schemes such as non-existent stock offerings, high-tech investment opportunities, and credit-repair services.

Some of the con artists on the net are those who have used telemarketing, infomercials, newspapers and magazines, and normal mail to attract consumers to their products, services, or investment schemes. In turning to the internet, they have found a cheaper way to reach millions of potential new victims. This is the darker side of the internet, where the ability to find out someone's identity would make fraudsters think twice.

Types of online advertising
Most of the questionable online advertising falls into one of two categories: classified advertising or disguised advertising.

▶ *Classified advertising.* Classified advertising has the greatest number of questionable ads. No matter where you look in classified ads online, chances are they will contain some false and misleading claims. For example, many classified ads promote quick and easy weight-loss products or programs that don't work. Another hot area in the classifieds is 'business opportunities.' The traditional work-at-home schemes, such as stuffing pillows or mailing envelopes, have been replaced by offers to use your home PC to 'make money fast' in your spare time. Other ads encourage you to invest in communications technologies, such as making money by recruiting other people into a 'high income' scheme of some kind (pyramid selling). Again, the marketers' promises on these investments are likely to be false.

▶ *Disguised advertising.* Disguised advertising is hard to recognise because it is not clear that something is being advertised. Disguised ads usually come in the form of a recommendation from someone, often by email or on Usenet. The comments or statements about the quality or the performance of a products or service may be ads in disguise.

A variation is where you apparently receive an email message by mistake: the message contains some vital advice to buy a certain kind of stock or product because the sender of the message has inside knowledge. Such as 'Jim, I've just found this new software called 'Zapit' that will let you call anywhere in the world for free!' You are not Jim but, then, the sender of the message knew that but didn't care – the same message was probably sent to thousands of other people who were also not called Jim. The sender, of course, owns 'Zapit' and 'Zapit' is probably a fake program or even a virus. Emails are rarely sent to the wrong people, especially if they contain what seems to be such good news.

Hoaxes and chain letters

Hoaxes are usually minor threats to your security but can also be extremely annoying and, at times, a cause of extreme embarrassment. They range from the simple April fool type of joke to a complete web site designed to fool you into giving them money. The most common type is the chain letter that either warns you to spread the email onto x more people 'or-else' or those that promise you a reward after forwarding the message to five friends. The only result of your labours will be angry emails from those you forwarded the message to.

Chain letters

A chain-letter hoax well known amongst internet 'oldies' is the M&M email message:

> Hi. My name is Jeffrey Newieb. I am a marketing analyst for M & M's chocolate candies based in Hershey, Pennsylvania.
> As the year 2000 approaches, we want to be the candy of the millennium - As you may already know, the roman numeral for Y2 is MM. We are asking you to pass on this email to 5 friends. Our tracking device is calculating how many emails you send out. Everytime it reaches 2000 people, you will receive a free case (100 individual 55 gram packs) of delicious M&M candies.
> That means the more people this reaches, the more candy you're going to get.
> Mmmmmm ... yummy M & Ms the year 2000!!
> Remember, nothing but no M & M s will come your way if you do not share this with at least 5 people.

Needless to say, even if you do forward the emails on, there will be no sweeties for you. Any email that asks you to send the same message to a number of people or asks a number of people to send mail to one person is almost certainly a hoax. Send a polite email to the sender of the message telling them that it is a hoax, then delete it.

Hoax virus warnings

A more worrying form of hoax is the virus warning that a friend forwarded to you. The fact that it came from a friend makes it particularly believable. Unfortunately, that is how chain letters operate and virus warnings have become one of the new kinds of chain letter. But what if it is a genuine warning? How do you tell? See one of the following sites:

http://www.drsolomon.com

http://www.datafellows.com

http://www.datarescue.com

http://www.metro.ch/avpve

Fig. 26. Data Rescue is one of many companies that will try to rescue the data on your hard drive if the data gets badly corrupted by a virus. Provided you take precautions, you may never need their services.

Hoaxes can cause frustration and a lot of wasted time but some hoaxes are far more malevolent than most because they are designed to do harm in some way. This type of hoax is covered in the section on harassment on page 93.

Auction scams

In September 1999, CNN reported that online auctioneer eBay some-times inadvertently hosts some pretty unbelievable proposals. These often generate a few bids before being discovered and taken off the site. Some examples included the auctioning of a young man's virginity, the sale of more than 75 human kidneys, and several babies. After the incident, sales of kidneys and babies have been banned from the site and referred to the law enforcement authorities.

'Certainly there's room for people to be funny on the internet, but I think people need to exercise good judgement. There are transplant pa-

Fig. 27. eBay is one of the biggest auction sites on the internet, selling just about anything you can imagine. People have even tried to auction such things as tear-gas, children, and their 'best' friends.

tients waiting years for a kidney. To them, this is not a joking matter,' said Steve Westly, eBay's vice president of marketing.

One seller, however, said he wasn't kidding when he added an auction entry that read 'Health conscious, fully functional kidney, 30s male with daily intakes of spring water, vitamins and exercise.' He included the requirement that the buyer must pay hospital and travel expenses and that the hospital must be 'top of the line'.

Earlier in 1999, eBay also banned the sale of guns and ammunition after items advertised included missiles, rocket launchers and other military weapons. The list of items banned from the site also includes human remains, live animals, counterfeit items, false identification documents, explosives and police identification.

Case studies

RealJukebox gathers data on its users
A company was caught in a controversy when it was discovered that its software used a 'globally unique identifier', along with information about what music tracks that you listen to, post codes and email addresses, to identify users. The software (RealJukebox) was designed to allow you to store audio CDs on your PC's hard drive for later playback. But it was discovered that the program also collects and monitors users' personal information and sends it to RealNetworks without the user's knowledge or consent.

The company admitted collecting information surreptitiously, and later announced that it would 'stop transmitting any information that is attached to individuals.' Still, many users said they would delete RealJukebox from their computers.

Why would a music company want to snoop on your listening habits? For the same reason as any of the violations discussed in this book: because your personal data is very valuable to them. One report said that marketers in the US are paying between 10 cents and $2.50 for profiles of consumers, often based on their zip code and buying habits.

Comet tracks hardware serial numbers
In November 1999, the *Wall Street Journal* reported that Comet Systems tracked people's movements on the web. Comet did not inform the 16 million users that the free cursor software tracks their movements on the web and collects their hardware serial numbers. The software transforms a computer cursor into cartoon characters and other images.

ISP Publishes user names and passwords
In 1999, a Dundee-based ISP called 08004u published the personal details of around 200 users on the web after 'a lapse in concentration'. Names, addresses, user names, passwords and other sensitive information were published when technicians switched servers. According to 08004u, the information was only visible for five minutes and contained the details of 40 or 50 people. *The Register*, an online news service, reported having received a copy of the list that contained personal details on some 200 subscribers.

Email reveals the Iran-Contra scandal.
The Iran-Contra scandal was uncovered due to email messages being discovered. Oliver North had deleted the damning messages from his own system, not realising that they were also stored on central computer files.

The Big Business Eye
In June 1999, online marketing company DoubleClick acquired Abacus Direct, a Colorado direct marketing firm, for well over a billion dollars. Abacus had a database with information on over 80% of US households. It is likely that DoubleClick intended to merge the information from the two databases. The CEO of Abacus, Tony White, said: 'The goal is to have the most complete picture of the consumer you can.'

Bank details sold
Early in June 1999, the State of Minnesota sued the US Bank for allegedly selling social security numbers, account balances, and other sensitive customer data to a telemarketing company in exchange for commissions. Apparently several other banks in the USA are selling customer information.

Credit Information published on the internet
A report showed that an American financial company revealed the financial records of up to 1.5 million South Africans. The records included names, addresses and identities, telephone and mobile phone numbers and bank account details.

Woman sacked
In June 1999, *The Times* reported that Lois Franxhi, an information manager for a management consultant firm, was sacked for surfing the internet during work time. She was apparently trying to check travel arrangements for a holiday. Although she filed for unfair dismissal on sex discrimination grounds, she lost the case after it was ruled that she was guilty of misconduct.

Store cards used to threaten customer
In a large supermarket in the USA, a man slipped and fell on spilt yoghurt in the dairy section. He threatened to sue the store because he broke his knee. The store, which uses 'loyalty cards' similar to many UK supermarkets, told him he had better not take legal action because of his history of regular purchases of alcohol, which they had on record and would use in court against him.

3 Hackers, crackers, criminals and cons

In this chapter we will explore:

▶ *attacks by email*
▶ *password sniffing*
▶ *social engineering*
▶ *the abuse of children*

The boundary between hackers and crackers is fuzzy but the most precise difference is in intent – hackers break into computer systems in order to point out the weaknesses to the owners whereas crackers seek to exploit the weaknesses for some kind of gain or to create damage. Many of the larger IT companies employ hackers to test their systems and others often issue a prize to the first hacker to break into a system. Hackers perform a service, crackers seek to exploit or cause damage.

Small businesses have much to fear from the hobbyist cracker: the young internet-savvy person who has a grudge to bear or friends to impress. Attacks on smaller businesses that use the internet are becoming more common – recently, an estate agent had its web site defaced: hard pornography pictures replaced the usual pictures of houses.

Its not just estate agents that are at risk – any business that uses the internet is vulnerable to attack by anyone with a little internet knowledge. Software distributors, news services, online banking services – all are at risk. Some are more secure than others but attackers can be very sophisticated and, if successful, devastating to an unprepared business. In October 1999, for example, someone hacked the web site of stationery giant Staples and redirected browsers to their major competitor. On 30 Nov 1999, Staples announced that it filed a lawsuit against its assailants claiming damages for lost business and for the recovery effort.

More than half of the companies which took part in a computer crime

Fig. 28. 'Big Brother is Watching.' The Hacker News Network supplies news of interest to hackers and anyone interested in privacy and internet security.

and security survey in the USA reported unauthorised access by people from inside their organisations. 60 per cent said that internet-based attacks were becoming increasingly problematic. The figures were published by Computer Security Institute (CSI) and the FBI. The cost of unauthorised access is estimated to be over $125 million, according to the companies in the survey. An up-to-date list of 'cracked' sites is at http://www.attrition.org/mirror/attrition/index.html. The list of sites on one hacker site for November 1999 numbered over 600 and included

Mastercard Austria
Homes and Loans Inc
Australian Broadcasting Authority
Missile Interaction Service Research
Monica Lewinsky's site (cracked four times in the same month)
Our Lady of Lourdes Catholic School
EMAP Online
Supreme Headquarters Allied Powers Europe (SHAPE)
NATO Airborne Early Warning and Control (twice)
Moscow Bank
Chinese Ministry of Foreign Affairs
The U.S. Embassy in Bosnia
The British Army
… and many more

Defacing web sites may seem relatively harmless, but to gain access to a web site may mean that a username and password have been compromised. That username and password may also enable the attacker to access to other parts of the victim's network: accounting, personnel, or the research archive for example.

Home users are unlikely to come under threat from hackers simply because there is no real challenge for the hacker. There is no prestige in hacking into someone's family web site unless the attacker has some grudge. If it does happen, however, almost anyone with a basic knowledge of the internet can cause untold misery for a person or a family.

That the internet is a battlefield is obvious; you only need to read the papers to learn about the dangers of viruses, terrorism and child pornography. Internet crime is becoming more common and those in the know can use their internet skills to cajole, con, and even cause physical injury to people. You are one of the potential casualties. All the more reason to learn how to defend your privacy and security.

Attacks by email

You are vulnerable through email in many ways. However, the most common attacks are:

email bombs	list-linking	forgery
viruses	replay	switching

Bombs, list-linking and forgery are the most common because they need little knowledge on the part of the attacker. The last three need a good deal of expertise and are much harder to defend against. These attacks tend to be targeted at business systems, either to do wholesale damage or to surgically collect and alter critical information.

Email bombs

If one day you retrieve your email only to find that there are hundreds or thousands of messages from the same person, you have been mail-bombed. Email bombs are rarely dangerous but they can waste valuable time while you sort out the genuine messages from the bomb 'fragments'.

▶ *Email bomb* – An attack by email where you are sent hundreds or thousands of email messages in a very short period. This attack often prevents you receiving genuine email messages.

Your phone bill may also increase as a result of the longer download times. This kind of attack can be classified more as petty harassment than a security threat. The attacker is usually an immature person who dislikes you for some reason. Sending a mail bomb is made easier by programs specially written to automate the process.

In some cases email bombs can result in a denial of service: using email becomes impractical because of the large number of email messages you receive. You are 'denied' the use of email. Occasionally, the bomber is so persistent that the amount of messages becomes too much even for your ISP's computer to handle, and it crashes. If a bomber shows this kind of persistence, contact the police. It is likely that the harassment will someday overflow into 'real' life and may even result in death threats or worse.

Mail bombers often choose the time when you are away or on holiday so that your mailbox fills up. Once the number of emails waiting on your ISPs server reaches a certain level – the quota – the ISP's software will refuse to accept any more messages and return them to the sender as undeliverable. Such denial of service can be very messy and difficult to tidy up. But at least there are simple measures you can take to filter out any mail from the bomber, with the next kind of attack it is more difficult. See page 93.

List-linking

Sooner or later you will probably subscribe to an online news service or update service where you receive regular emails on a particular area of interest. *The Economist*, for example, offers a daily news update, and many other special interest groups have mailing lists. Some of the busier lists can send you hundreds of emails each day.

List-linking is a form of harassment where an attacker signs you up to as many lists as possible. The effect is a form of mail bomb, which can waste far more time and money than a conventional mail bomb. There are many different kinds of mailing list, and so there are many different ways of unsubscribing from the lists. Imagine trying to contact each one to cancel your subscription. Many of them may even want to charge you for their subscription. Imagine, one step further, that the person who is attacking you knows your credit card details. Again, there are packages

Fig. 29. Liszt holds a vast database of around 100,000 different email lists. You can search for the subject of your choice, then subscribe to receive regular information by email.

that can automate list-linking, so even a less determined attacker can easily cause havoc.

Forgery

Forgery is often the next stage in an escalated attack after list-linking because it calls for more thought and some creativity from the attacker. Where mail bombs and list-linking can be the outlet for a quick burst of anger, forgery is definitely premeditated and can be far more malevolent and damaging.

Forging a message entails using a false name and email address. Email messages contain header messages that contain information about who has sent the messages. All of the identifying features in the header (see page 96) of a message such as 'Return-Path' and 'From' can be changed. Most email programs allow you to alter the more obvious fields to read whatever you want – the technicalities of forgery are fairly simple.

The next step is to write the message or Usenet post so that people believe it has been written by the intended victim. Spammers and junk emailers also tend to forge email messages so that their true identity can not be found out.

Viruses and Trojan horses

A computer crash never seems a danger until it actually happens – then it can be too late. Your computer crash may be the result of a normal program fault or of a hardware failure such as a bad disk or a power surge. However, a crash can also be caused by a computer virus and if this is the case, the damage may be far more difficult to repair if possible at all.

A biological virus, like the flu virus, is very small and highly infectious and can multiply only in living cells of animals, plants, or bacteria. A computer virus is similarly very small and 'infects' computer programs or documents by attaching itself to the larger program. Once attached, they replicate themselves and infect other programs.

The first viruses were called 'worms' and were created accidentally. A worm developed on the early computers when engineers first learned how to run programs simultaneously. Programs sometimes overstepped

Fig. 30. Doctor Solomon's anti-virus software has been around for a while and is regarded by large companies as one of the best. It is easy to use, and regular updates are available. You can have it running all the time in the background while you work, both offline and online.

their boundaries and damaged data in other parts of the system. This damage occurred at random, much like woodworm attacking a table. Hence the term. Eventually, a worm called the Xerox worm spread over a network to other machines. This was the beginning of the computer virus.

Modern viruses, however, can do far more than just make copies. Many viruses are designed to disrupt the normal operation of the computer, or to damage and delete files. The 'payload' can be as harmless as a silly message on the screen, or as disastrous as a completely corrupted hard drive. Some of them, polymorphic viruses, are as difficult to detect as a stealth bomber: they can change themselves and blend in with the normal files of your computer to avoid detection by anti-virus scanners. Others take over the computer and disable any anti-virus measures you take. Many of the worst kind of virus use a time delay in which they replicate invisibly as much as possible until a certain 'D-Day' then they all 'blow up' at once. By that time the virus may have infected many thousands of files and many computers. Viruses must not be underestimated.

There are three main categories of virus, classified by how they spread:

▶ *Program viruses* – These viruses spread from file to file, attaching themselves to many different kinds of program. When you run a contaminated program, the virus will load into the computer's memory. Once there, it can infect or cause damage to other programs. It's rather like a person with flu sneezing in a crowd.

Fig. 31. Dr Solomon offers online support.

▶ *Boot sector viruses* – The boot sector is a special part of a disk (floppy disk or hard disk) that contains a set of instructions used by the computer whenever it is switched on. Boot sector viruses alter these instructions to take over the computer. When a floppy with an infected boot sector is placed in a new machine the virus can then copy itself onto the boot sector of the hard drive. Boot sector viruses only infect a computer if you leave the floppy disk in the drive when you turn the computer on.

► *Macro viruses* – Most modern business or office software allows the use of complex macro languages to automate common tasks or to simplify complex ones. A macro virus is stored within a document or template. When you open an infected document, the macro virus is activated and infects your system. From then on, each document you save is infected with the macro virus. Those documents continue to spread the infection every time someone else opens the document.

The Melissa virus, for example, is one of many that use Microsoft Word's in-built macro language to cause damage to documents. Other Word Processors can also be affected; in fact any program which allows advanced macros may be susceptible to viruses. Macro viruses are widespread at the moment due to document sharing in larger companies.

Another virus, BubbleBoy, is not as widespread as Melissa but just as dangerous, if not more so. The virus may affect users of Outlook Express. Microsoft says: 'To date, the virus only exists in a laboratory setting and has not harmed any customers. The virus is embedded within an email message in the HTML format and does not contain an attachment. Microsoft recommends that any customers who receive an email with the subject heading 'BubbleBoy is back' should delete it immediately and empty their deleted items folder.' In Outlook Express the virus is activated if the Preview Pane is used to view the contents of the email. The virus causes no damage apart from forwarding itself to all addresses in your address book.

Fig. 32. Microsoft warns about the BubbleBoy virus, one of the latest email viruses. It will email copies of itself to people in your address book. It is irritating, if relatively harmless compared to some other viruses. All viruses should be avoided like the proverbial plague.

These viruses are particularly troublesome for businesses because they affect word processor documents. Once an infected document is loaded, every new document or spreadsheet opened can also be corrupted.

---

http://www.microsoft.com/Security/Bulletins/bubbleboy.asp

Microsoft®
Security Advisor   All Products | Support | Search | microsoft.co   *Microsoft*

rity Home | New Headlines | Bulletins | Partners | Events & Training

BubbleBoy Virus

Last updated: November 10, 1999

Microsoft recently became aware of the existence of a new virus called the BubbleBoy virus that may affect users of Microsoft Outlook and Outlook Express. To date, the virus only exists in a laboratory setting and has not harmed any customers. The virus is embedded within an email message in the HTML format and does not contain an attachment. Microsoft recommends that any customers who receive an email with the subject heading "BubbleBoy is back" should delete it immediately and empty their deleted items folder.

In Outlook, a user must open the email for the virus to spread, and in Outlook Express the virus is activated if the Preview Pane is used. This is not a malicious virus, but will send itself to all addresses in every address book the user has access to in Outlook. Customers can take the following steps to protect themselves from this virus:

▶ *The Trojan horse* – A Trojan horse is not classed as a virus, because it does not usually reproduce itself. It is a malicious program disguised as a normal one such as Windows Calculator or in fact any kind of program you can imagine from a game to a financial package. The real purpose of a Trojan horse is to either cause damage to the victim's computer or to eavesdrop and collect information such as passwords or credit card details.

A Trojan horse is frequently sent via email with the claim that it is a software upgrade. Recently, several people have sent forged emails that contain so called Microsoft software upgrades to people on the internet. Be warned, very few companies – including Microsoft – ever distribute software directly via email. Common ways that Trojans are disguised are:

1. Posted onto to a newsgroups with a claim that it is another program
2. Included or referenced in a spam message
3. Placed on a genuine-looking web site
4. Sent by instant messenger programs or chat systems such as ICQ, AIM or IRC.
5. Disguised as an email from an ISP or computer software company (like AOL or Microsoft) with a hoax message asking somebody to run a program (for example a software update).

Large companies know better than to send software by email. Microsoft, for example, warns users against Trojans by saying:

'We distribute software on physical media like CDs and floppy disks. We do distribute upgrades via the internet but when we do this, the software will be available via our web site, http://www.microsoft.com, or through our FTP site, ftp://ftp.microsoft.com. We occasionally send email to customers to inform them that upgrades are available. However, the email will only provide links to the download sites – we will never attach the software itself to the email. The links will always lead to either our web site or our FTP site, never to a third-party site.'

Replaying of emails
Replaying is the interception of a message and sending one or more duplicates. For example if an email message authorising payment of £100 to an account was intercepted, it could be duplicated and sent repeatedly resulting in multiple payments of £100 to the same account. This kind of attack is the realm of the hi-tech criminal and is rarely encountered by the home user or small business. However with the increasing use of internet banking by home computer users, replaying bank transactions may soon become more of a risk.

Switching of emails
Switching is technically the hardest attack to make. An email message is intercepted and carefully changed to alter the meaning before being sent

back on its way to the genuine recipient. For example £10 could be changed to £100. This is technically difficult to pull off because a message usually has to be intercepted, changed, and sent on its way again in seconds.

Password sniffing

Sometimes it is possible for a person to gain access to an ISP's system and leave a program running that eavesdrops on the internet traffic that is passing through. The program, called a sniffer, intercepts and records usernames and passwords.

▶ *Sniffer* – a network analyser whose name originated from a product called the Sniffer. This product was manufactured by Network General Corporation to isolate problems with network communications. A password sniffer is placed on the computers of an ISP by a hacker or cracker and collects passwords.

Password sniffers are a common attack on ISPs. A sniffer can capture thousands of passwords. For example, in 1994, a network sniffer was placed on several internet systems and collected more than 100,000 user names and passwords. You as the user have no direct protection against this kind of attack apart, from regularly changing your passwords and making sure your ISP updates its system with the latest security patches as soon as they are available.

Fig. 33. Windows will remember your dial-up password and username if you let it. This can be handy for you, but it also means that anyone else with access to your computer can connect to the intenet and assume your identity (email name etc).

Social engineering

Social engineering is a term used on the internet for falsely gaining an individual's confidence in order to gain some personal information. For example, if someone telephones you claiming to be a customer services representative, or some kind of official from your ISP, and asks for your password, they are trying to socially engineer your password.

Social engineering is one of the main tools of hackers and computer criminals. If they can convince someone that they are genuine and are only asking for information that they can be trusted with, many people will be willing to give away details that would otherwise be closely guarded. It is in fact much easier than you would expect, especially if the 'engineer' knows a name or two already. If you received a call from someone who claimed to be acting for your boss and used the boss's name, would you have the courage or loyalty to refuse? Would you care? Many would not.

Hackers, crackers, criminals and cons............................

The abuse of children

Few cases of child abuse resulting from the internet have been reported. Some incidents may go unreported because the children do not feel able to discuss them with parents. Children may become involved in many types of harmful incidents: from being tricked into revealing information about their personal life, to something as serious as kidnapping and sexual abuse. The internet can give disturbed people the confidence to do or say things that otherwise would be impossible to get away with in a normal social environment.

As soon as children are able to use a computer keyboard and connect to the web, they are at risk from unscrupulous web sites or individuals. Teenagers are more at risk than younger children because they often use the computer unsupervised, and are more likely to take part in online discussions regarding companionship, relationships, or sexual activity. See page 122 for advice on protecting your children.

Fig. 34. The British rock star Gary Glitter was prosecuted and jailed for four months for possessing child pornography downloaded from the internet. He had sent his computer to be repaired. The repair staff looked at personal files on his computer, and then reported him to the authorities.

Legal and financial risks for children

There is also the risk of a child being tricked into doing something that has negative legal or financial consequences. Children may unwittingly give out a credit card number – yours maybe – or do something that is illegal in some way. If the child is using your email account, you may be the one in court for libel or worse. For example, many would-be hackers are teenagers who fail to realise the risks of what they are doing. At the very least, a careless word here or there could result in legal action being taken against you or your child.

One very popular kind of site you may want to keep your children away from is the online auction. The combination of a child, a credit card, and an online auction is enough to make any parent shiver (see the case study at the end of this chapter). On the internet, there is no way to know a person's real age, nor can you tell if a credit card is in the hands of the rightful owner or a rebellious 13-year-old. The control must, therefore, be exerted in the home on your own computer.

The scenario becomes more sinister when you realise that not all companies are going to use the web for purely ethical purposes. There have been cases where companies have targeted children and used private information about them to gain their trust and thereby get them to do things that they would not otherwise do – such as find and give out credit card and address details of the parents. No child would give away credit card details to a stranger, but what if there was an animated cartoon frog on the site that called the child by his nickname? It has been done.

Aggression and harassment
There are parts of the internet where children could come across people with very extreme views, and may suffer prejudice, hatred, threats and harassment. The internet gives voice to people of all types, some of them actively engaged in violence or illegality of some kind. Some of them only need the slightest provocation to make them harass or stalk someone using the internet – children are not exempt from this kind of threat and are more vulnerable.

Pornography
Another risk to children is that they may stumble across pornographic material. No matter how high the penalty for illegal pornography, there will still be places on the internet where there is a risk of coming across it by accident.

Many children come into contact with 'porn mags' smuggled into school, but the internet makes the possibility of abuse far more dangerous. It may start with a known paedophile pretending to be a teenager – girl or boy – and offering to swap pictures of himself for pictures of your child. Of course, the pictures will not be of himself but of some other innocent child. If a rapport develops between your child and the imaginary friend, the pictures may well become highly pornographic in nature. Weeks later, though, it will be you who will hear a knock on the door, and you who will be caught with child pornography on your computer.

Molestation
If a trusting relationship develops, a child might be manipulated or tricked into providing personal information or arranging a meeting that might result in danger to the child or family members. In some cases, children have been tricked through email, bulletin boards, or chat areas. Paedophiles have used alternative identities to gain a child's confidence, then arrange a face-to-face meeting. The case of photo-swapping above may develop such a bond of trust between the two 'children' that yours is lured into a secret meeting that you will be unaware of until it is too late.

These are worst-case situations, but make no mistake, there are serious threats to your children out there on the internet – and what child can resist having secrets from their parents? Your child may think that the secret friend is a 16-year-old, but is it? Take the following imaginary scenario as a warning. It is set in an internet chat room.

Trudy: Hi there!
John: Hello
Trudy: Where do you live?

Entertainment > Humc
- **Sex**

Regional > Countries
- **Sex**

Society and Culture >
- **Sex** Crimes

Society and Culture >
- Oral **Sex**

Society and Culture >
- **Sex** Work

Hackers, crackers, criminals and cons..

John: Ashton, what about you
Trudy: Hey, I live there too, on Church Street, what street are you on?
John: Market Street, number 25
Trudy: Cool!

Sounds innocent enough, doesn't it? But a 'Church Street' can be found in almost any town, and what if 'Trudy' was in reality a 50-year-old male paedophile? Would you realise that a paedophile had actually gained access directly to your child's bedroom (where some children's computers are)? Think about that then turn to page 122.

Case studies

Hotmail hacked
In September 1999 Paul Cronin was head of penetration testing at a network security company called Century.com. He said that people should stay away from free web-based email services, or risk leaving themselves open to hackers and viruses. He made the claim after hackers broke into Microsoft's Hotmail servers and published details of how to retrieve information from system's 40 million email accounts. This is not a new situation – there have been a number of security exploits over the past two years. Free web-based email services should not be used to send any sort of confidential information.

The eight hackers in Sweden at 'Hackers Unite' claimed: 'We did not do this hack to destroy, we want to show the world how bad the security on Microsoft really is'. Microsoft PR claimed that 'very advanced knowledge of web development languages' was needed to accomplish the hack, but Richard Smith of Phar Lap said 'It's trivial, it's just some HTML code.' Just nine lines of code.

Globalnet system crashed by spam
In August 1999 the large ISP, Globalnet, was the target of a spam attack from Florida. As result, all email was delayed for almost a day while the spam was cleared.

ISPs turn against spam
In April 1999, for the first time, two UK ISPs took legal action against junk emailers. The first, Virgin Net, filed suit against bulk emailer Adrian Paris for sending more than 250,000 unsolicited email messages using his Virgin Net account. The lawsuit sought damages for breach of contract and trespass. Despite a warning, Paris set up new accounts and continued sending thousands of messages.

In an even more extraordinary case Bibliotech, an ISP in London, took legal action against a spammer in the USA. Benchmark, an Atlanta print company, allegedly subjected Bibliotech to hundreds of unsolicited commercial emails with forged return addresses. Benchmark offered to pay damages to the ISP and to refrain from further violations against Bibliotech. But Bibliotech was not satisfied and demanded that Benchmark should promise not to subject other ISPs to the same kind of spam. Bibliotech spokesman Chris Verdin said, 'As long as spam-related settlements protect only the complaining ISP, there will always be another target for the spammer.'

Eventually, the wording of the agreement stated that 'the spammer expressly acknowledges each and every ISP in the world is an express third-party beneficiary of the agreement.'

Bank customers panic

In July 1999, a 24 year-old was arrested because he sent forged email messages from his Hotmail account urging customers of the Columbian Davivienda Bank to take their money out because the government were about to take over the bank's affairs. The resulting rush of withdrawals amounted to around $11.4 million in a single day.

Bank details stolen

Emir Feisal, editorial accountant of *The Sunday Times*, wrote an article[1] describing his astonishment and difficulties after the discovery that his credit card number was being used to buy thousands of pounds worth of products in America, including over £700 with Amazon Books. After many telephone calls and letters, he tried to cancel his credit card. Only after he admitted to working for *The Sunday Times* did he get any kind of reasonable customer service from the credit card company. Emir concluded that it was an internet site that must have directly or indirectly provided the criminal with his details.

Security sites attacked

In August 1999 Symantec's web site was attacked. Days later the web site of AntiOnline, another internet security site, was attacked. The attacker redirected visitors to a web page with the image of an eye and the message: 'Expensive security systems do not protect from stupidity.'[2]

Harassment

Jayne Hitchcock is an author who fell victim to a vicious attack because she complained about a person's online conduct. Jayne's ordeal began with a complaint against a literary agency and escalated into a comprehensive campaign of harassment – from email bombs to death threats and worse (real stalking and physical violence).

The story began in 1996 when the agency posted an innocent-looking ad to the Usenet newsgroup 'misc.writing'. It said that the literary agency was looking for writers to present to publishers. Jayne, knowing nothing about this agency, sent in a book proposal after talking to a person calling himself James Leonard on the phone. Within a week she got a response praising her proposal and asking for a $75 reading fee. Luckily, Jayne knew this was not usual practice for literary agents. Jayne wrote back to the agency and reminded them they had not previously mentioned fees of any kind – the agency returned her manuscript.

Jayne began to warn other writers about the agent's unexpected charges. In April 1996, other writers joined in the protest and warned everyone who enquired about this agency's adverts on Usenet. Doggedly and profusely, however, the agency continued to send hundreds

1. 'Shop at Your Peril on the Internet', *Sunday Times*, p. 7, 8 August 1999.
2. *San Jose Mercury News*, 6 August 1999.

of duplicated ads in almost every newsgroup in Usenet. By now, the true nature of the agency was becoming clear. The agency began to use free trial accounts with ISPs such as America OnLine, Prodigy, and Netcom. The ISPs cancelled its accounts but as soon as one account was disabled, another one would be opened.

The heat was turned up on Jayne when someone started to forge posts so that they appeared to come from Jayne's email address. The text of these postings was clearly intended to cause a massive response to the supposed poster. Hundreds of these messages began appearing in many newsgroups, including 'misc.writing'. A group of volunteers, including network administrators, began an active campaign to stop the spam. The worst attacks were when the forged messages claimed she was interested in sado-masochistic sexual fantasies with the members of extremist newsgroups: the messages contained Jayne's actual phone number and address.

By January 1997 most of the forgeries had been stopped, but the agency's normal spam continued. Jayne's lawyer filed an aggravated harassment suit against the agency, and on 22 January papers were served at the place of business of the agency in New York. Since harassing Jayne, the agency has been kicked off more than twenty internet service providers for spam – including IBM, IDT, Prodigy, AOL and Compuserve. One account was used to focus on the newsgroup 'misc.writing', with over 200 posts spammed to that single newsgroup in less than two days. Quite a few were, ironically, complaints about spam.

The extent of the agency's malevolence was revealed when Jayne's lawyer received a threatening phone call during the case. 'The man then asked if I were John Young and, after I confirmed that, asked if I were handling the case for Miss Hitchcock,' Attorney Young relates. 'After I also confirmed that, he said to me, "You'd better drop that case – or I'll come and fuckin' kill you." When I asked "And who might you be?" I got a click.'

Part Two: Defending yourself

. . . .

▶ *Comment* – The internet's 'anarchy' may seem strange or even unnatural, but it makes a certain deep and basic sense. It's rather like the 'anarchy' of the English language. Nobody rents English, and nobody owns English. As an English-speaking person, it's up to you to learn how to speak English properly and make whatever use you please of it (though the government provides certain subsidies to help you learn to read and write a bit). Otherwise, everybody just sort of pitches in, and somehow the thing evolves on its own, and somehow turns out workable. And interesting. Fascinating, even. Though a lot of people earn their living from using and exploiting and teaching English, 'English' as an institution is public property, a public good. Much the same goes for the internet. Would English be improved if the 'The English Language, Inc.' had a board of directors and a chief executive officer, or a President and a Congress? There'd probably be a lot fewer new words in English, and a lot fewer new ideas (Bruce Sterling).

The internet is anarchistic, but not necessarily lawless. According to the *Oxford English Dictionary*, the word anarchy comes from a Greek word meaning 'without a chief or head'. There is no implication of a lack of order or justice, just a different mechanism. What is happening on the internet has never happened before. A completely new kind of culture is growing in which practically the whole planet is beginning to work together. Millions of independent human beings are communicating directly across international barriers and creating a revolution on a larger scale than the industrial revolution.

Governments will learn that members of their societies will be less inclined to meekly obey. Internet users will more and more question government decisions. Despite their bureaucratic instincts, governments will be forced to become more accountable and open. Secrets will become harder to keep, mistakes harder to cover up. Technology has made it possible for the ordinary person to outmanoeuvre governments, to break through the barriers and walls that their countries would otherwise put in front of them. The speed of the internet means that even if you could stop one person from releasing information, it will probably already be too late.

Our requirements for secure and productive use of the internet fall roughly into four areas. Consider the following table:

	Information in	*Information out*
I want	Access to information.	Free speech.
I don't want	Spam and other types of harassment or invasiveness.	Violation of private email and other information.

It is perfectly reasonable to expect that you can find information on the internet. After all, that is the sole reason to connect onto the internet for some of us. All of us use information regularly on the internet. The enemy of access to information is censorship.

1. Free speech is essential if we are to fight oppression of any kind, including in our own country.

Defending yourself ....

2. Spam is unwanted because it is never requested, and the cost is borne by the receiver. In this way, it is unlike the junk mail we get through the post.

3. Just as we expect our private letters not to be read, the same applies to email messages.

The main purpose of Part Two is to show you how to defend yourself against the 'I don't wants' of the above table, without threatening the 'I wants'.

4 Walls have ears: good practice

In this chapter we will explore:

▶ *curbing those bad habits*

▶ *beefing up your passwords*

▶ *stop giving away your private information*

▶ *making Outlook Express safe*

▶ *how to silence your browser*

▶ *protecting against virus infection*

▶ *learning to trust web sites*

▶ *case studies*

. . . .

Many of the defences in this book are highly effective. Even a highly skilled attacker would have trouble breaking through if the techniques are used properly. On the other hand a moment's carelessness can make your system so vulnerable that not even a child would find it difficult to break in. Any security system in the world can be compromised by a moment's carelessness. More systems are compromised because of human error than by hackers or crackers.

Curbing those bad habits

A password is the key to your privacy and security: anyone that has the key can get in. A password is useless if you tell every one what it is. That may sound obvious but there are many ways that you can unknowingly give your password to thousands of people.

Passwords

Walk through any large office and you will come across computer monitors decorated with little yellow post-it notes. It is frightening how many of those contain the user's passwords. That kind of carelessness is an open invitation for any passer-by to log on to your computer and gain access to your personal work. You might as well leave a signed letter of resignation on your desk or, if it is a home computer, leave your wallet on the front doorstep. If you must leave passwords written down, at least leave the wrong passwords. There's only one place for a written record of your password, the bin. Oh, really?

Don't throw any piece of personal information in a bin without first making the information illegible. If hackers, law enforcement organisations, or even nosy neighbours want to snoop or gain surreptitious access to your computer system, one of the first places they will look is the rubbish bin or skip. Waste paper can contain information such as names of those in your family, dates of birth, and much more. At work, information about the network setup and sometimes even usernames and passwords are thrown out without being shredded or burned.

Even if the information does not give away passwords, some of it could be used to work out weak passwords, or to enable someone to use social engineering. For example if a hacker found out the network security officer's name, he could call people in the same company pretending to be the security officer and then ask employees for their usernames and passwords 'to sort out some problems'.

A possible example of social engineering
'Hello, Mr Johnson, this is Ken Jenks, the security officer for XYZ Ltd. We've got a crisis here and I'm having to phone all of the employees in your section. The problem is that we have lost our backups due to a power failure and in order to recover the information we need to log on individually as each user.'

'Yes, we're going to be here all night at this rate. If you would be kind enough to tell me your user name and password, I'll backup your data straight away, otherwise one small power surge and you will have lost a weeks work.'

Laziness is also a bad habit which can open your system to dangerous tampering. Do you use the same password for different things? Don't. The password you use, for example, to gain access to an online web site may not be secure and only saved on the server in a text file that is accessible to others. If that password is the same as your dial-up password or network password at work, you are at risk.

▶ *Important* – Never tell your password to anyone, even friends. Those friends may not deliberately give your password, but are they as security conscious as you? They will probably make some of the mistakes described in this section or even give your password to another who tells it to … you get the idea.

Beefing up your passwords

A password can be compared to the key of a padlock just as some locks are easy to open with a bent piece of wire, some passwords are easy to guess. A weak password is like a key that is left under the doormat – an invitation to anyone. Hackers, mischief makers and work colleagues can all take advantage.

Don't make the mistake of thinking that you have nothing to hide; there is often more at stake than having someone read your email or change your web site. Once someone has discovered your password, they then have access to an alternative identity. To all appearances, they are you. If they send an insulting email message; if they try to break into a bank's computer system; if they want to swap child pornography with others they can do it all in your name. It is going to take some fast talking to explain to the police why, for example, a person using your internet account has just replaced the Queen's portrait with a picture of a half-undressed supermodel.

Password-cracking software is freely available. It tries thousands of passwords tirelessly and relentlessly until it gains entry. Once a program such as this is set to work, it will typically guess a weak password in under a second. It is estimated that 20% of passwords can be worked out in seconds.

Rule 1: your password should not be obvious.
Some of the most common passwords are:

password	your login name
god	your street or house name
love	your name or a variation of it
genius	the name of someone you love
hacker	a car license number or model
sex	a special date or time
qwertyuiop (top row of the keyboard)	

Do any of those sound familiar? If you use any of these, change it. What do you change it to? Where can you find a password you can remember but which others will not be able to work out? One method is to think of a phrase that you are familiar with or one that you can easily remember. It could be a line in a song, a joke's punch-line, a famous quotation – anything that is easy to remember but not something that others will associate with you. Its no good using a phrase that is framed next to your desk or on your screen saver, or a line in a song that you often sing to yourself. Choose something neutral or very private. For example, one of the books on the shelf in front of me is *The Oxford Dictionary of Quotations.* You could use the title to help with a password.

▶ *Tip* – Choose one of the longer words in the phrase or title such as Dictionary and adapt it by substituting some letters for numbers. It may be 'D1ct1onary' or 'Qu0tat10ns' or '0xf0rd' (two zeros).

Another easy method is to take a phrase of eight or more words. Then use the first letter of each word. For example, 'look before you leap' would become 'lbyl'. Using methods like this, you can make passwords that are easy to remember but difficult to guess. Now you have a word that is not associated with you, is it safe? No, look at rule 2.

Rule 2: Passwords should be at least eight letters/digits long.
The more letters in a password, the more attempts a password cracking program would have to go through (as long as it is not in the list of common passwords). If you used a one-letter password, the program would have to try up to 26 combinations. For a password with two 'places' you would have to multiply the two numbers. For example, a two-letter password with lowercase only would make the program try up to 26 x 26 combinations, 676 combinations in all. The table carries on from here.

So you see, with eight letters, the task of the password-cracking program is huge. You may be surprised to hear that even the level of security that an eight letter password gives you could be cracked – don't be, there are some very powerful computers out there. Safe yet? Not yet. We should make passwords far more secure by observing the next rule:

Rule 3: Passwords should combine numbers and letters and upper and lower case.

Walls have ears: good practice ....

In general you should always ask yourself 'could my password be found in any dictionary in any language?' If you answered yes, change the password because in some situations, password crackers can scan all of the words in even large dictionaries in a relatively short time. Adding numbers to the password ensures that it is unlikely to be found in any dictionary.

Most of us are lazy: we use easy to remember passwords that don't take much thought to type in. We only use lowercase letters and rarely consider numbers. Using uppercase, lowercase and numbers in our passwords makes them far more difficult to guess. Say you used a ridiculously easy password such as 'god'. By using the rule above, you could make even that pathetic password far more difficult to guess. An attacker would have a harder task to guess this one, even if he knew that you used the word 'god'. He may make many attempts before he found the right combination:

God	G0d	GoD	G0D
god	g0d	goD	g0D

By using upper case, lower case and numbers in passwords, we make it far harder for a password cracker. For one-letter passwords, the number of combinations is 26 + 26 + 10, which is 62. A password with two 'places' has 62 X 62 combinations or 3844; and with three 'places' it is 62 x 62 x 62 or 238,328. See the table below for comparisons.

	Combinations	
Number of places in password	Lower case only	Lower case, upper case and numbers
1	26	62
2	676	3,844
3	17,576	238,328
4	456,976	14,776,336
5	11,881,376	916,132,832
6	308,915,776	56,800,235,584
7	8,031,810,176	3,521,614,606,208
8	208,827,064,576	218,340,105,584,896

A password of eight letters has a large amount of possible combinations but not so many that a powerful computer could not find a password if given enough time. However, with the combination of upper case, lower case and numbers, the task would be far more difficult. To make it even tougher to crack your password, you can use computer-generated 'random' passwords. On the web, you can find sites that use Java applets to create random passwords.

Stop giving away your private information

Clear those Usenet archives
Usenet is only one of the many places on the internet where you give away information about yourself but it is probably the most accessible:

anybody with a browser can compile a dossier on you from your posts. Usenet is public and anything you post to a newsgroup and the date you posted it will be recorded for a very long time. With this in mind, the only way to prevent your posts from being archived is to say nothing. But there are times when you just have to speak out. So, how can you minimise the amount of information that is kept?

You can prevent companies like Deja.com (see page 28) from storing your posts by adding the text 'x-no-archive:yes' to the headers of your outgoing messages. To do this in Outlook Express, simply type in 'x-no-archive:yes' as the *first* line of the message – it will not work if it comes later in the message. Using this header ensures that when services such as Deja scan the Usenet posts, yours will not be archived. However, if somebody includes your text when they reply to your post, your words may be stored in the archive as part of that others person's messages. Is there a way around this? Only one: say nothing you would not want on record.

If you have posted messages previously that you want to remove from the Deja archive follow this link to remove or 'nuke' those messages:

http://www.deja.com/forms/nuke.shtml

No matter how innocent and neutral your posts to Usenet are, your privacy will still end up being abused. Junk mailers use archives like Deja.com and also scan the newsgroups themselves to harvest email addresses. All it needs is one post and you will be marked: your email address will be in large numbers of junk mail databases. Why? Because with every Usenet posting you make, you are broadcasting your email address to the world. Each message you send contains information that is usually hidden in a part of the message called the header (see page 98). This usually includes your real name and email address.

To give you a little protection from junk mail, you can change this information so your messages contain a pseudonym or an altered email address. Most junk mailers use programs to harvest email addresses and these programs can be fooled so they collect an invalid email address – one which will not result in you receiving the junk. Many internet users alter their address so that people with genuine replies can work out the address but an automatic program will not. My address:

admin@ukwriters.com

could be altered to read:

admin@NOJUNKukwriters.com   or
adminATukwritersDOTcom

Both those would fool the programs, but humans would know to take out the 'NOJUNK' or, with the second example, replace the 'AT' with @ and the 'DOT' with a full stop.

How to nuke a me

1. Using the entry file
   the message you w

   Note: Without ex
   currently receive m
   an old email addre

2. Select the target n

3. Choose the messa

4. Click on the "nuke

Walls have ears: good practice ....

▶ *Action* – To change your settings in Outlook Express, click 'Tools' and 'Accounts'. Then select the news tab and highlight the news server you want to check. Now click 'Properties': in the 'General' section, you will see what name and email address is sent with every post to Usenet. Altering these will help to keep your mailbox clear of junk and will add a layer to your privacy.

The web site giveaway

The world wide web is the most wonderful part of the internet. Home pages can open your life to people with similar interests; they can help your love life or job prospects, or simply keep friends and acquaintances informed. If you are a small business, the benefits are obvious.

But web sites can also supply information to the more predatory members of the internet. There's no point in fitting the latest burglar alarm to your front door if you leave the side door open: that's asking every con artist and criminal that passes by to come in and help themselves. Likewise, if you publish personal details on a home page, there's no point in taking any action to protect your privacy because you will not have any. Some of the problems that can be caused by publishing details on your home page are:

1. email harassment

2. junk mail

3. discrimination

Almost every home page will bring in some unwanted email from people offering you a way to make money quickly by first paying them or, if you are a woman, lustful emails from men with bad manners and half a brain. The better known the site is, the more attention it will attract good and bad. If you are unlucky, it could result in email harassment on a large scale (see page 67).

Are your views controversial?

If you have controversial views of any kind, publishing them on a home page that identifies you can lead to harassment or discrimination. Even if your site does not identify you, your web space provider may be forced or conned into identifying you. In some countries, the consequences may be prison or worse but even people in a less repressive country such as the UK, for instance should be aware of the potential dangers. The more anyone knows about you, the easier they will be able to manipulate or exploit you. The con man that has seen your web site may know what your hobbies are and what you look like and may be able to put enough information together to identify you and where you live. Remember that bosses also browse the web and that curiosity may lead them to your site: are your views, say on politics or company policy, going to get you sacked?

Clearly you should not have to hide away but a sensible compromise is to carefully vet the content of your site and minimise the weaknesses.

Consider omitting your phone number and address – both email and snail. If you need an email address on the site, you could include it as an image not as text so that the junk-mailers' scanners will not be able to pick them out. Those of you with fairly large sites should keep your email address to just one page: a 'contact me' page and link to it from the other pages. If you have the facility and the knowledge, use a form instead of a hyperlink. Forms are more difficult to scan for email addresses.

▶ *Hyperlink* – a phrase or image that calls up another web page when you click on it. Also just 'link'.

If you have a political or human rights message to get out to the world, consider using Usenet instead of the web. You are likely to reach a larger number of people and can more easily keep your anonymity (see page 111).

Pentium III serial numbers
After much protest from privacy organisations, Intel has released a utility that will let you disable the processor serial number. The utility is a Windows program that enables or disables the reading of the processor serial number by software. This allows you to control which software programs or web sites have permission to read the processor serial number. Once installed, the utility runs automatically each time your computer is turned on. The utility places an icon in the system folder that provides a visual indication of the state of the serial number feature. You can disable the

Fig. 35. Intel releases a control utility that you can use to turn off the serial number of the Pentium III processor. Some people say that it can be easily bypassed by snoopers.

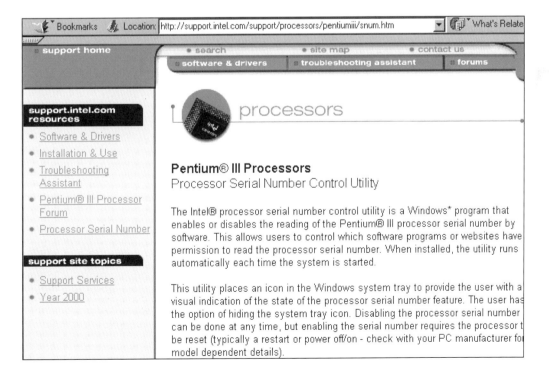

serial number at any time, but enabling it requires a reboot in most systems. To find out more, visit:

> http://support.intel.com/support/processors/pentiumiii/snum.htm

If you want to protest against the Pentium III serial number, the only choice is to buy nothing from Intel, or visit Intel's online forum and submit your comments at:

> http://support.intel.com/nowogroups/pentiii.htm

or email them at: support@mailbox.cps.intel.com.

You might even email AMD, a competitor of Intel that does not have a tracking serial number programmed into the CPU chip, at:

> http://www.amd.com/support/email.html

Express your concern about Intel's plans, and encourage them to resist any pressure to introduce a tracking number. And, finally, when buying a new computer, tell the salesperson that you specifically want a computer that contains an AMD processor.

Go manual: turn off the features you don't need

1. Internet Explorer version 5 has a facility which can remember your logon names and passwords for web sites. If a thief steals your computer, this is just one more way that they can do damage to your reputation. Turn this feature off.

2. AutoComplete was designed to make it easier to fill out online forms by providing a drop-down list of items that you have previously entered in a particular text box on a web page. When you select an item, it is automatically put into the field. The feature is very useful on its own, but its real power shines through when the benefit is transferred between web sites. Common elements such as names, telephone numbers, and email addresses won't have to be constantly retyped because they will have already filled in this information on someone else's site. The main point – if you insist on keeping AutoComplete turned on – is never to let anyone else use Internet Explorer 5 on your machine, because they might be tempted to use your personal information when filling in forms.

3. Although not a risk on the internet, your browser also creates a history database. This stores every place you've visited, and every filename and picture element you've seen on the web. The history database is particularly vexing in IE4 and IE5 as these browsers time and date-stamp everything and then save it in separate tracking folders. These can identify your activities down to the second you were there, along with details of each page seen.

4. Consider disabling page hit counting in Internet Explorer (Tools, Internet Options, Advanced) to stop web sites recording your visits. Coun-

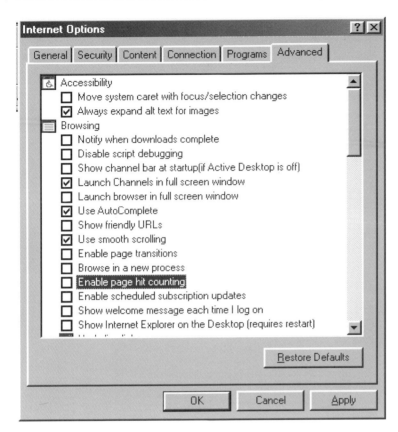

Fig. 36. Internet Explorer lets you disable page hit counting where your visit, including details such as your IP address, is logged by a web site.

ters will be incremented but normal logs will not record anything about you.

Make Outlook Express safe
Getting security set right in an email reader like Outlook Express is very important, because today most harmful content is distributed via email. It is claimed that Outlook Express can be configured to offer increased security, but the current versions make it difficult to work out how to do this. The problem is that Outlook Express security is dependent on Internet Explorer and, if you have them, Microsoft Office programs. Outlook Express can only be made secure by a complicated set of precautions involving Outlook Express, Internet Explorer and Office.

▶ *What to do* – Adjust your security settings within Outlook Express itself in Tools, Options, and clicking the Security tab. There you will find that you can set Outlook to use one of two security zones: Internet and Restricted sites zone.

By default, messages are viewed in the internet zone. Here, messages that contain JavaScript code, ActiveX controls, or Java applets are automatically executed when a message is read. So almost all of the problems associated with scripts and ActiveX components can be abused in an HTML email message.

Fig. 37. Message options.

Walls have ears: good practice ....

Fig. 38. Outlook Express only gives you two choices in its security zones section to improve your defences. Change the settings in Internet Explorer as well.

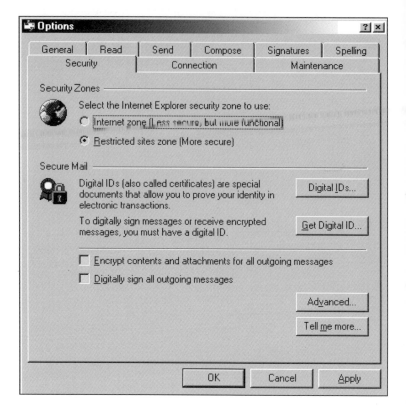

The second security zone, Restricted sites, turns off ActiveX and Java support and supposedly offers greater security. However, it still allows JavaScript to run and Microsoft Office documents will still open without any warnings. A malicious person can send you a message with a line or two of script that opens a browser window, and, incredibly, that window is then run in the internet security zone and can thus run harmful Java and ActiveX controls. Alternatively they can send you a Word document infected with a macro virus. If you have not configured Word properly, your computer will be affected.

▶ *Action* – To make Outlook Express safe, change the settings within Internet Explorer, Word, and Windows Explorer (see page 82)

How to silence your browser

End the scripts
What can users do about all these different security holes? One approach is to download patches to fix security holes as they are found. Unfortunately for most users, it is not possible to find or keep up with the latest patches. Will you know what patches you need? It might mean going to four or five different web sites regularly, just to see which security patches are available.

Most malicious scripts activate themselves when the web page loads, so action after the fact is not effective. You must disable scripting before

80

you connect to dubious sites. It is far easier to protect yourself than it is to repair the damage after an attack. If you don't believe that there is any danger, go to Richard M. Smith's page and test your system for vulnerabilities and run a few demonstrations that may persuade you to be a little more careful:

http://www.tiac.net/users/smiths/acctroj/axcheck.htm

Do you disable JavaScript, Java, VBScript or ActiveX? The decision is a balance between how much you value your privacy and security and how much fun you want to have on the internet. If you have sensitive or valuable information of any kind on your computer, disable them all; otherwise disable them according to the table below:

1. ActiveX   Should be disabled by all but the bravest.

2. VBScript   Not enough is known about VBScript, and few sites use it, so it would be safer to disable it.

3. Java   Can be considered safe for most home users.

4. JavaScript   Mostly harmless, but be sure to back up your data regularly.

How to turn off ActiveX and Java in Internet Explorer 4

1. In Windows Start menu, select Settings, and then Control Panel.

2. Double-click on the internet icon in the Control Panel window.

3. Select the Security tab in the Internet Properties dialog box. Select Internet zone.

4. Push the Reset button to make sure that the internet zone is at the Medium level.

5. Select Custom level for the internet zone.

6. Click the Settings button in the Custom level.

7. For the setting 'Script ActiveX controls marked safe for scripting' in the Security Settings dialog box, check the Disable option.

8. To disable Java, scroll down to Java Permissions and check the Disable option. If you do not wish to disable Java, you should get the Microsoft JVM update which fixes a very serious hole in the Java capabilities of IE4. The Microsoft update can be downloaded from http://download.microsoft.com/download/javasdk/install/3186/w9xnt4/en-us/msjavx86.exe

9. Click the Ok button in the Security Settings dialog box.

10. Click the Ok button in the Internet properties dialog box.

Walls have ears: good practice ....

How to turn off ActiveX and Java in Internet Explorer 5.

1. In the Windows Start menu, select Settings, Control Panel.

2. Double-click on the Internet Options icon in the Control Panel window.

3. Select the Security tab in the Internet Properties dialog box.

4. Select the Internet zone

5. Click the Custom Level button.

6. Scroll down to 'Script ActiveX controls marked safe for scripting' in the Security Settings dialog box and check Disable.

7. Click the Ok button in the Security Settings dialog box.

8. Click the Ok button in the internet properties dialog box.

Fig. 39. You should change the security options in Internet Properties. You can get there from Control Panel or Internet Explorer by Tools, Internet Options, then Security.

Now return to the test site above and see how your security has improved. Ironically, if you put a site on the 'Restricted sites' list, the 'Run ActiveX controls marked safe for scripting' option is enabled by default. As described earlier, even some controls marked as safe can be made to cause damage to your system. Before you add any sites to the 'Restricted sites' list, make it safe by performing the same steps as above, but for step 4 select the 'Restricted sites zone'.

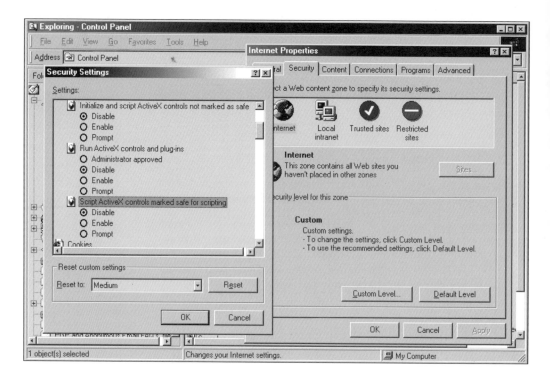

Crunch those cookies
Disabling cookies is simple in both main browsers.

▶ *In Internet Explorer* – Open theTools menu, then Internet options and then click on the Security tab. Click the Custom level button and once you are into the security settings, scroll down to the Cookies section and disable both per-session and permanent cookies. Click OK then OK again. Your browser will no longer accept cookies. However, web sites will still be able to access the cookies already on your computer.

▶ *In Netscape Navigator 3.0 and up* – Go to the Options Menu, select Network preferences, then select the Protocols tab. Locate the section Show an alert before and check the box labelled Accepting a cookie.

▶ *In Netscape Communicator* – Go to the Edit Menu, select Preferences. When the preferences window appears, select the Advanced section and tick Disable cookies.

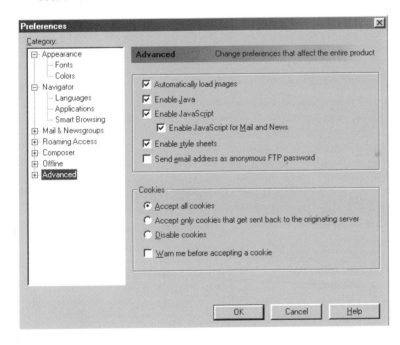

Fig. 40. Cookies can be disabled in Netscape so that you are not tracked as you browse the web. Just click 'Disable cookies'. You can also easily edit your preferences so as to disable the running of Java and Javascript.

If you prefer the convenience of cookies for some sites but resent the intrusion from some other sites, there are a few good programs that may help, called cookie cutters. They will give you far greater control so that you can select which ones to accept or reject. Cookie cutters are listed on page 140.

Another method, which may work for some cookies, is to edit the contents of cookie text file and replace the ID information and everything after the domain entry until the asterisk, with space characters. No information, no tracking. The change seems to stop sites making modifications to cookies and placing new cookies. And that way you can keep the useful cookies if you want to.

Clear that cache and history list

▶ *Action* – In Internet Explorer 5 you can clear your cache by selecting Tools, Internet options. Click the General tab, and then click the Delete Files button. To clear the history file, click the Clear history button on the same page.

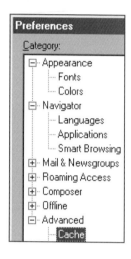

▶ *Action* – In Navigator 4 choose Edit and Preferences. Then select Cache under the Advanced branch, and click both the Clear Memory Cache and Clear Disk Cache buttons. To clear the History list, select the Navigator branch, and then click the Clear History and Clear Location Bar buttons.

If you are using a computer on a company network, this precaution is probably futile anyway because your every move on the internet is recorded somewhere. There is little you can do about this.

Home users may be unable to avoid their tracks being recorded by their ISP unless they use some of the anonymous services explained later in the book.

Protecting yourself against virus infection

A computer virus can easily destroy days, months or years of work, yet still we often fail to take sensible precautions. The mere mention of viruses puts fear into our hearts but not, it seems, into our minds. Even the most seasoned professional will occasionally ignore the advice that he throws around, and lose work that he has not backed up. If you insert disks into your computer, open email attachments, share disks, or download files from the internet, you are likely to meet viruses. But one precaution you should take right now is to get some virus scanning software. Once you have installed it, update it frequently new viruses appear every day.

Anti-virus software
Anti-virus software – virus scanners – may be almost as old as viruses, but no virus scanner is foolproof. For practical reasons, anti-virus software is designed only to scan for the most common viruses. Therefore aim for software that promises regular and frequent updates. And get the latest updates. If you do this, or better still if you use two scanners from different companies, you can be fairly certain that all known viruses will be detected. Good anti-virus software should:

1. Be up to date – get the updates as soon as they become available.

2. Conform to standards set by the National Computer Security Association.

3. Be able to scan floppy disks, hard drives, CD-ROMs, and network drives.

Fig. 41. F-Prot is one of the best anti-virus program for home users and it's free. There are frequent updates.

4. Be able to monitor your computer while you are working, so it can warn you if you try to open an infected file.

5. Include a version of the scanner that can be run on a bootable floppy disk.

Where do you get it?

One of the best scanners is F-Prot, written by Fridrik Skulason in Iceland. 'The English language shareware version of the program, is available directly from Iceland,' Says Fridrik, 'This version of the F-Prot anti-virus program is free of charge for private use (that is, free for any individual or family using it on a personally owned computer).' If you have internet access, you can download the latest (at time of writing) F-Prot from:

http://www.isvr.soton.ac.uk/ftp/pc/f-prot

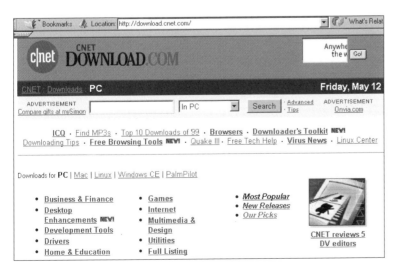

Fig. 42. Download.com offers lots of useful programs including F-Prot and many of the other software programs mentioned in this book.

Walls have ears: good practice ....

At another site, http://www.download.com, you can download other free anti-virus software such as Disinfectant for Macintosh, and trial versions of commercial anti-virus software.

Most anti-virus software scans your computer's memory soon after you switch on. The software should display a warning if you try to open an infected file. Once an infected file is identified, most virus scanners will ask you if you want to clean the infected file or, if it cannot be cleaned, to delete it. Let the scanner clean or delete the infected file. Don't be tempted to ignore its existence or you will end up with many more infected files. Deleting is perhaps the safest option – you have got backups, haven't you?

As soon as you get an anti-virus program, make a copy of the bootable floppy, or make one and write-protect the disk. Keep it in a safe place away from dirt, children, pets and sources of magnetism such as television sets, speakers, and computer monitors.

▶ *Stealth viruses* – If any anti-virus company claims that its program is able to detect any stealth virus, it is no more than a marketing trick. The only foolproof technique to detect stealth viruses is to cold-boot the computer; turn the power off then on, using a clean write-protected bootable floppy to make sure no virus is present in memory. Then check the computer for viruses.

Infected file attachments and file downloads
One of the main causes of virus infection is the file download. The precautions for most files (except Office documents) are simple but must be strictly followed:

1. Don't open downloaded or attached files. Save them first. Scan them with an up-to-date virus scanner before running or opening them. It may help to create a special 'quarantine' directory or folder on your hard drive for this purpose.

2. If you have changed your browser's settings so it can automatically open downloaded files, disable it now. It may be a little inconvenient but it may save you hours of work or even dismissal from your job.

3. Back up your files regularly and keep the backup disks in a safe place. Even though computer viruses are not airborne, this will help to keep the disks free from viruses. If a virus infects your system, clean it then restore your files.

Some other actions that will make life a little less nerve-racking:

4. If you regularly receive documents by email attachment, ask for them to be sent as plain or rich text format to avoid the risk of macro viruses altogether.

5. Similarly, when you want to send a document to someone, send it as a plain text or Rich Text File.

Dealing with macro viruses

Virus scanners can detect macro viruses once they have infected a document, but by then it may be too late. Preventing infection takes just a couple of steps. Make sure your Office programs are set to warn you before running macros contained within documents. By default, Word and other Office programs do display warning messages whenever you open a document that contains macros. You can then choose to open the document with its macros disabled. Many macros are safe, but make sure you trust the sender of the document before you run any macros that it contains.

▶ *Action* – To enable the macro protection in Word 97, Start Word and open the 'Tools' menu. Select 'Options' and then the 'General' tab. Click on 'Macro virus protection' and make sure it is checked. If you accidentally let a macro virus run even once, your system may have had the virus detection turned off.

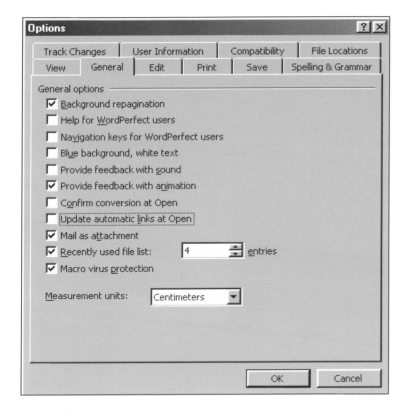

Fig. 43. MicroSoft Word has an in-built protection mechanism against macro viruses. The protection is turned off by default. Before running a macro, Word warns you, and asks whether or not you wish to proceed.

Gagging Office documents

By default, Internet Explorer will give you a security warning before launching a downloaded application or file, so the risk of virus infection is small. Unfortunately, if the file you download is a Microsoft Office document you will not get the warning. Office documents were seen as safe and that one would contain a virus was unthinkable until someone wrote the Melissa macro virus.

Regardless of the security settings in Internet Explorer, Microsoft Office documents will still be opened automatically when they are downloaded or included in an email message. This poses a threat of infection by macro viruses. If you have macro protection turned on, there should be no damage, but one further step you can take to minimise the risk is to prevent Office documents from automatically opening by adjusting the settings in Windows Explorer (*not* Internet Explorer):

1. Double click on the My Computer icon on your desktop.
2. Click on the View menu.
3. Then Folder Options ...
4. Click the File Types tab.
5. Scroll down and find any reference to Office programs: Microsoft Word or Excel. Then, one by one ...
6. Select the file.
7. Click the Edit button.
8. Check the Confirm open after download option.

Fig. 44. If you download a file from the internet, you are usually asked whether you want to run it, save it, or just open it for viewing. However, some Microsoft files are exempt and will open and run automatically. To find out how to stop them, in Windows Explorer click View, Folder Options, then File Thypes.

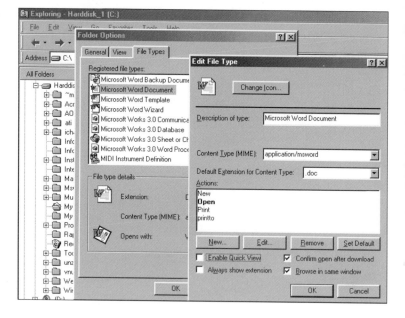

That will prevent Office documents opening automatically in Internet Explorer or Outlook Express when they are viewed. Flaws do exist that might allow a malicious macro to run without warning, even if you did have the macro virus protection turned on (see http://www.microsoft.com/security for more information). These have not been generally exploited, but all it needs is one virus to get through and it might have turned the macro-virus protection off.

Microsoft has released a patch that does practically the same as the steps above. It ensures that opening any Office document (Word, Excel, PowerPoint or Access) from Internet Explorer will cause a warning to be displayed. You can download this patch from:

   http://officeupdate.microsoft.com/downloadDetails/confirm.htm.

Oops, too late!
Sometimes a virus sneaks by all of your defences. It may have come from a game loaned to your children, or from the illegal software that nobody will admit to having put there. Whatever the cause, it has happened. Stop everything, *now*!

1. Calm down. The virus has probably not destroyed your hard disk, but throwing the computer out of the window will.

2   Get two cardboard boxes. Use big letters and mark one box 'UN-TESTED' and the second as 'GOOD' or 'TESTED'. You will not need a third box labelled 'BAD' – use the bin for the infected disks that you can't clean.

3. Do a strict search of your house – toy cupboards, briefcases, secret pockets get every floppy disk you can find.

4. Find the bootable floppy that came, or that you created, with your virus scanner.

5. If you have no virus scanner, try to find and keep aside one bootable floppy that you are sure is clean. This is the crucial starting point, you must be certain that it is clean. Put the rest in the box marked 'UN-TESTED'.

6. Do a clean reboot. Turn off your computer, count to ten, and with the clean and write-protected bootable floppy in the drive, start it up again.

7. Run your anti-virus software. Find and if possible repair the infected files on your hard disk. If the damage is too great for the software to fix, delete the files and replace them with clean backups. Test the back-ups.

8. You may also have to re-install some of your software. Check the in-stallation disks for viruses before you do.

9. Now check the floppy disks. Check them carefully one by one. When clean, put the disk in the 'GOOD' box. This way, if you are interrupted during your cleaning operation, you will at least know where to resume your purge. Destroy and bin any disks you can't clean.

10. Finally, to prevent a future disaster install the virus scanner to work in the background so it guards your computer as you work. You might even consider keeping the computer locked away.

Walls have ears: good practice ·····································

Fig. 45. Hoaxes may not cause direct damage, but they can cause you to act rashly and needlessly cause unintentional damage. Check the CIAC site before taking the extreme measure of reformatting ('wiping') your hard disk.

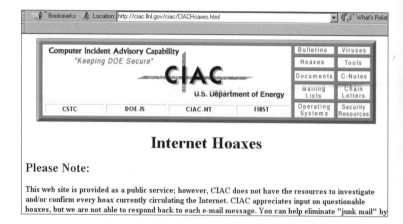

Myths and hoaxes

Panic spreads easily, especially by email, and all that is needed to start the flood is one misinformed philanthropist warning all his friends and acquaintances about an email virus. The virus, they say, will erase the files on your hard drive or cause other damage if you read the email. Of course, those friends and acquaintances will also pass the message on. Thus the panic spreads. Of course, now that everyone is talking about it, there must be something in it. Is there?

The Computer Incident Advisory Capacity (CIAC) says of hoaxes: 'Since 1988, virus hoaxes have flooded the internet. With thousands of viruses worldwide, virus paranoia in the community has risen to an extremely high level. It is this paranoia that fuels virus hoaxes. A good example of this behavior is the 'Good Times' virus hoax which started in 1994 and is still circulating the internet today. Instead of spreading from one computer to another by itself, Good Times relies on people to pass it along.'

How do you identify a hoax? There are several signs:

(a) If the warning sounds as if it is has been sent by an official organisation, or uses overly technical terms, it is probably a hoax because virus warnings are rarely sent to individuals unless part of a regular newsletter or mailing list.

(b) Be especially alert if the warning urges you to pass it on to your friends. This should warn you straight away to be careful.

(c) If the warning says that it is a Federal Communication Commission (FCC) warning, it is a hoax. The FCC has not and never will send warnings on viruses.

Always double-check before embarrassing yourself and clogging up the internet. Any of the usual news sites or mailing lists will pick up straight away on new viruses. The CIAC site above is especially useful in that it documents the hoaxes circulating around the internet as well as the genuine risks. Another useful web site is the Computer Virus Myths home page which contains descriptions of many known hoaxes:

http://www.kumite.com/myths

Learning to trust web sites

TRUSTe was founded by the Electronic Frontier Foundation (EFF) and the CommerceNet Consortium. Its mission is to 'build users' trust and confidence on the internet and, in doing so, accelerate growth of the internet industry.' TRUSTe is probably the most active and most respected organisation concerned with privacy and commerce on the internet. Their rationale is that respecting the privacy of the online public is essential for businesses.

'TRUSTe believes that an environment of mutual trust and openness will help make and keep the internet a free, comfortable, and richly diverse community for everyone. As an internet user, you have a right to expect online privacy and the responsibility to exercise choice over how your personal information is collected, used, and shared by web sites. The TRUSTe program was designed expressly to ensure that your privacy is protected through open disclosure and to empower you to make informed choices.'

Simply put, if a web site uses information about you, it must describe how it uses that information in an easy-to-understand manner. This description, written in a privacy statement, will contain at least the following:

1. What information is collected.
2. How it will be used.
3. Who it will be shared with.
4. What choices are available to you regarding how the information is used.
5. How the information is protected.
6. How you can update or correct the information.

The most important feature of TRUSTe is its trustmark. This is an online seal of approval similar to many trade seals you see in the UK. The trustmark is displayed on the web site of the scheme. It is awarded only to sites which follow the privacy principles it recommends.

Trustmark: The TRUSTe seal that is awarded to web sites that keep to the privacy principles outlined below and agree TRUSTe oversight. The principles include:

▷ Adoption and implementation of a privacy policy that takes into account consumer anxiety over sharing personal information online.

▷ Notice and disclosure of information collection and use practices.

▷ Choice and consent, giving users the opportunity to exercise control over their information.

▷ Data security and quality and access measures to help protect the security and accuracy of personally identifiable information.'

The site owners must also agree to comply with TRUSTe oversight.

Walls have ears: good practice ....

Case studies

New computer virus
An email virus named Bubbleboy was the first of its kind. The virus can infect a system simply after the message subject line has been highlighted. Those using Windows 98 and 2000, and some versions of Windows 95 with Internet Explorer 5.0, and Outlook Express are susceptible to infection. Netscape products apparently will not let the virus through. The effect of Bubbleboy is to rename the infected computer'o registered uoor to DubbleDuy. No other damage is caused but the method used to activate the virus could be used to activate far more damaging viruses.

Check your Usenet dossier.
Go to the Deja.com power search page at http://www.deja.com/ home_ps.shtml Enter your email address into the keyword box, then click the 'Search' button. If you have posted anything to Usenet without the x-no-archive header set, you will see them listed in front of you. You may also see replies to your post that contain your email address in their reply. My search came up with over 700 posts by me and more than 2,000 other posts which contained my email address – enough to show up on any harvesting program used by junk-mailers. If you have an unusual name, try the same search using your name. Sometimes it is amazing what you will find.

Furthermore, if you have registered with Deja, others can inspect your 'member profile'. This displays information such as a short bio and other personal and business information, and a picture if you have included one. Fine for actors and other people in the public eye, but would you really want every criminal on the internet to see that information?

▶ *Author profile* – a summary of all the Usenet messages from a single email address saved in the Deja archive.

Can you delete those references to your email address from the archive? Yes, to some extent: go to: http://www.deja.com/forms/nuke.shtml/ 'You must submit a request for each message that you want nuked.' When Deja receives your request, they send you an email. Once you reply to it, Deja will delete that stored message. As you can imagine, if you have hundreds of messages stored the process becomes very tedious and time-consuming, so better to prevent the archiving from the start.

Netscape vulnerable
A security expert encountered a vulnerability in the Netscape Navigator configuration file. A script can be placed on a web site to attack the Netscape preferences file. This file contains much sensitive information such as username and password for email and FTP, recently visited URLs, and more. The attacks try to locate the preferences file, execute it (it's a JavaScript file), and send the information to a desired location. If successful, the attack is completed in seconds and is invisible to you.

5 Protecting your privacy

In this chapter we will explore:

▶ *fighting the invaders*

▶ *using encryption*

▶ *PGP: strong encryption*

▶ *using digital signatures*

▶ *maintaining privacy at work*

. . . .

Fighting the invaders

Unwanted email is unwanted whether it is spam, UCE, or a hoax. Some techniques work for all kinds of junk, others are more specific. Rest assured, there are effective measures you can take whatever type of junk you receive. If you follow the advice in the good practice section in the previous chapter, the amount of UCE you receive will be minimal. However, persistent junk and harassing messages can still sometimes get through. If you only ever get one or two junk email messages, simply delete them. When the numbers increase, come back to this book and read on from here.

Most UCE is generated by people selling some kind of 'get-rich-quick' scheme; they ignore the usual marketing conventions instead hoping that the greater the number of messages, the greater the number of customers. The bottom line is: treat all ads or unsolicited emails ads with scepticism and never part with any money or personal information based solely on information obtained from a single source in any medium print, broadcast, or online.

The fact that almost everyone hates junk email escapes the attention of junk mailers. Reasoning with this kind of person is impossible. Thousands of people have tried, with no effect other than to be bombarded with even more UCE or insults and even harassment. Many people have

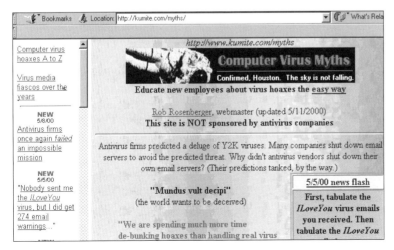

Fig. 46. Kumite is another site that deals with virus hoaxes. As it points out, more time is spent dealing with false alarms than with real viruses.

been mail-bombed by junk mailers in response to complaints and one or two have even received death threats.

If you receive a hoax forwarded by a friend, send a polite reply indicating the error of their ways and referring them to one of the hoax sites. If the email is a junk advert or, worse still, an insulting flame, the more you respond the worse it will become. Attempting to reason with the sender rarely works. Instead, apply some of the techniques outlined below. If one technique doesn't work, move onto the next more effective technique until the junk stops.

In my experience, there are only two methods that have any effect in stopping junk email. One is to filter it out. The other – for those of you who are really angry – is to go for the jugular.

Using mail filters

To guard against harassment or unwanted email adverts, one way is to 'kill' or filter out the attacker's email messages. This technique will also work with Usenet posters that annoy you.

Most email software allows you to set filters that will control your incoming messages and allow you to redirect, copy, delete, move and perform many other functions with your email. The most important use in the context of this book is that filters can protect you from unwanted messages, say from a junk email advertising company that persistently sends you requests for money.

A mail filter is a way of recording what kind of emails you want to skip over. To filter messages, you specify criteria to use to kill them. These criteria can include:

1. a subject line
2. part of a subject line
3. articles from one poster or from one site
4. cross-posted articles
5. follow-ups to other articles

You can sometimes also kill messages with a particular string in the body of the message.

How to change your filtering rules

In Outlook Express and Netscape Messenger, you can block messages from a particular sender or a domain, so that no email or news messages from that sender or domain will arrive in your Inbox or in the news messages you read. You can also add filters to act on messages according to what is in the body of the message. Outlook Express will also allow you to filter messages according to the size of the message, and whether it has an attachment.

How do I kill postings from a specific person?

To block or filter out a particular person, set the filter to scan the FROM: field for that person's email address. In Outlook Express 5, simply highlight the junk message then click the 'Message' menu, select 'Block

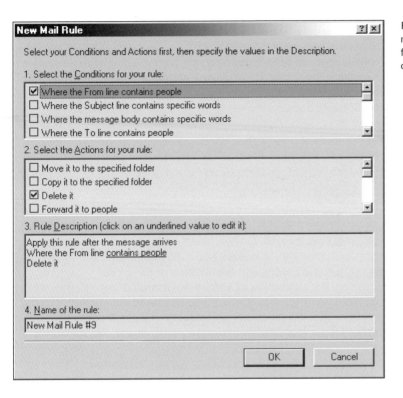

Fig. 47. Outlook Express mail rules enable you to filter incoming mail and delete any junk mail.

Sender'. In Netscape Messenger, add a message filter to delete all emails from that person.

How do I kill messages from a specific site?
Again, you would use the FROM: field, but to include *any* email address from that site you could use a more general filter that looked for the domain name of that site. For example you would filter out and delete any message that contained the domain name of the sending company or organisation.

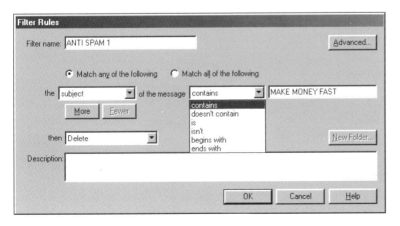

Fig. 48. Netscape also lets you deal with unwanted incoming mail if you know what word to filter on. Iopen up Netscape Messenger and go to Edit, Message Filters.

Protecting your privacy ....

Going for the jugular
Sometimes, the best way to strike back at these people is to hit them in the Achilles heel: their ISP. ISPs often have strict policies prohibiting the sending of unsolicited email, and will act swiftly by imposing fines, warnings, or by cutting the offender's access to the internet. Their reaction will be more final if the offending email message has been forged or contains verbal abuse.

What to do when you receive unsolicited email:
1. Always confirm that it is in fact unsolicited.
2. Identify the real sender if possible and their ISP.
3. Send off your complaints.

Check whether it is from a mailing list that you subscribed to while you were browsing the web. You may have forgotten that you subscribed or another person might have used your computer to subscribe to the mailing list. If it is a mailing list, unsubscribe in the proper way if you no longer want to receive the messages. Most mailing lists include instructions with each message. If you do decide to send a complaint, be polite, or at least civil. The person receiving your complaint is not usually responsible for the spam and may hate it as much as you.

Identifying the sender of an email and who to complain to
Look in the header of the message to see if there is an address where you should send complaints. Some ISPs include special lines in the header such as those for NetscapeOnline and Freeserve:

X-Report: Report abuse to abuse@netscapeonline.co.uk

X-Complaints-To: abuse@theplanet.net

If there is an abuse header, send your complaint there. If not, you may have to do some guesswork. Look at the sender's email address, e.g. molly@madasafish.com, and you can be sure that in most cases the ISP is identifiable from what comes after the @ sign – in this case, Madasafish. Some other examples are included in the table below.

Email address	ISP	Abuse address
someone@somewhere.demon.co.uk	Demon	abuse@demon.net
someone@somewhere.freeserve.co.uk	Freeserve	abuse@theplanet.net
someone@free4all.co.uk	Free4all	abuse@in2home.net
someone@ukonline.co.uk	Ukonline	abuse@ukonline.net
someone@breathemail.net	Breathemail	abuse@vip.uk.com
someone@btinternet.com	BT	abuse@btinternet.com
someone@aol.com	AOL	abuse@aol.com
someone@tesco.net	Tesco	abuse@uk.uu.net

As you can see, most of the ISPs can be identified simply by looking at the sender's email address. Forgeries will be dealt with later on page 101.

> **From:** Planet Abuse Team **To:** molly@madasafish.com
> **Subject:** Re: Abuse of freeserve (ABUSE#33102)
>
> Thanks for your recent abuse report.
>
> We have traced and verified the account(s) that related to your report. They have now been dealt with accordingly.
>
> Cheers,
> Planet Network Abuse Team

Fig. 49. You may be surprised at the positive outcome of your spam complaint. Indeed, the ISP may have received hundreds of similar complaints. Experienced spammers expect to get kicked off an ISP very soon, so they try to send as many junk emails as possible in the shortest possible time.

Once you know their ISP, send a copy of your complaint to the abuse address. If it is not clear where you should send your complaint, send copies to various addresses at their ISP. For instance, always send a copy to postmaster@site. The Postmaster is traditionally the person who deals with problems or abuses. However, quite a number of sites don't have a postmaster address. So send a copy to admin@site as well, and, to be absolutely certain, to root@site.

As mentioned, some of the above email addresses may not be correct. For example, a given ISP may not have set up an abuse account. In such a case the email will be returned to you with an error message advising that there was no such user. But at least one of your email messages will find its way to the complaints department.

Often, you get a message sent by an autoresponder, briefly confirming that your email has been received. The message will normally tell you what steps are being taken to investigate your complaint, or details of who to send future complaints to. A great list of abuse addresses is held at:

> http://www.abuse.net/cgi-bin/list-abuse-addresses

If you have identified the sender's ISP, you can take a look at Abuse.net at http://www.abuse.net/ . 'The abuse.net system helps forward messages about abusive activity on the internet to people who can do something about it.' Abuse.net forwards messages from you to the most effective complaint handler at the ISP.

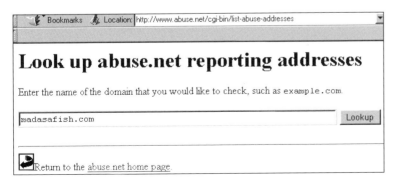

Fig. 50. If you are not sure who to complain to about unwanted email, consult the Abuse.net site. It has the complaint addresses for hundreds of ISPs.

Protecting your privacy ....

Many professional marketers and individuals who engage in bulk emailing unsolicited material are quite organised. Often they have their own internet domain name and hardware (such as mail servers and a direct connection to the internet). In these cases, it is unlikely that sending email to 'postmaster' etc at that site will remedy the problem. For example my own address is admin@ukwriters.com. A complaint to abuse@ukwriters.com or postmaster@ukwriters.com will be delivered to me and thus will have no effect – not that I would send you unwanted email messages!

Analysing an email message
Identifying who to complain to may not always be easy. For companies with their own domain name, you must analyse their header to identify who they get their service from. On other occasions, the mailer will know that they will annoy a large number of people with their junk mailing, so they try to hide their real identity to prevent a backlash. They use a business name, but give no street address or email details. Often they only give a telephone number, almost always an answering service, or simply a PO Box. Some detective work is required to identify who is behind the junk, and where the complaints should be sent.

To trace the email you need to analyse the header. Most mail readers do not show the header because it contains information that is for computer to computer routing. The only information you usually see from the header is the subject, date and the 'From' or 'Return' address. About the only thing in an email header that can't be faked is the 'Received' portion referencing your computer (the last received).

Showing the header in an email
The method varies according to the email program you use, but the following list includes most common programs.

▶ *Claris E-Mailer* – Under Mail select Show Long Headers.

▶ *Eudora* (before version 3) – Select Tools, Options, Fonts & Display then Show all headers.

▶ *Eudora* (versions 3.x, 4.x) – Press the BLAH button on the incoming mail message.

▶ *HotMail* – To expose the full message header, click Options on the Hotmail Navigation Bar on the left side of the page. On the Options page, click Preferences. Scroll down to Message Headers and select Full.

▶ *Outlook Express* – Highlight the email in your inbox (click once) and press CTRL-F3.

▶ *Netscape 3* – In the Netscape Mail window, click View, Document Source.

▶ *Netscape 4.xx* – Double click the message in your inbox. Click on View, Headers, All.

▶ *PINE* – Turn on the header option in setup, then just press 'h' to view the headers.

▶ *Pegasus* – Press CTRL-H'. This will show the full header's message, but will not add them to any reply or forward. Copy and paste the message into the new message to send these headers.

How to understand the header
If you are not sure where to send a complaint to, or the sender has set up his email software with a false email address, you can often still track down his ISP by analysing the headers.
Look at these headers for example:

```
Received: from post.corpex.com (post.corpex.com [195.153.3347.11])
      by yacko.t-rex.com (8.8.8+Sun/8.8.8) with SMTP id CAA26568
      for <molly@madasafish.com>; Fri, 12 Nov 1999 02:27:50 GMT
From: Bruce02@usa.net
Received: (qmail 2531 invoked by uid 6572); 12 Nov 1999 02:30:41 -0000
Delivered-To: bphjkh-admin@ukwriters.com
Received: (qmail 2528 invoked by uid 0); 12 Nov 1999 02:30:40 -0000
MBOX-Line: From usa.net!Bruce02 Fri Nov 12 02:30:40 1999 remote from mail
Received: from server02(p55.amax1.dialup.mkc1.flash.net[209.30.124.33]) (965 bytes)
by mail.corpex.com
      via smail with P:smtp/R:bind.hosts/T:smtp-filter
      (sender: <Bruce02@usa.net>)
      id <m11m6U3-003xmYC@mail.corpex.com>
      for <admin@ukwriters.com>; Fri, 12 Nov 1999 02:30:39 +0000 (GMT)
      (Smail-3.33.0.105 1999-Mar-3 #3 built 1999-Mar-26)
Message-Id: <m11m6U3-003xmYC@mail.corpex.com>
To: <admin@ukwriters.com>
Subject: Ready for a change? Not MLM!
Date: Sun, 31 Oct 1999 16:55:29
```

At first sight, you may get ready to send a complaint to abuse@usa.net because the message is from Bruce02@usa.net. But remember that it is easy to put a false from' address in any email program. Let's dig a little more.

The useful information is in the Received' lines. Received lines are like links in a chain and indicate the different servers that the message has been routed through. The message is passed from one computer to the next with no breaks in the chain. The final received line of the example above tells us that the message ended up at molly@madasafish.com (my computer) from post.corpex.com. My email account is with Madasafish but my email address is admin@ukwriters.com. I know that the information in that received' line is genuine and occurs in all of my messages.

The previous received line' shows that the message got to mail.corpex.com from p55.amax1.dialup.mkc1.flash.net or 209.30.124.33 in numerical terms. The numbers are just another way of indicating a domain name. Now this line is the first received line and so it gives you an indication of where the message comes from. Since this is the first received line, we know that it contains information about who the sender is. We can use that numerical IP address in the first received line

Protecting your privacy ....

(209.30.124.33) to give us more information.

Tools used to find people's identity: Whois
If you have an IP address, information about the person that owns that address will be listed in huge databases. Sometimes this will be an individual or a small company. At other times it will be an ISP or a government organisation. Whoever owns the number will usually be the person to complain to. You can search the databases with a service called Whois.

Using Whois, you can find out who the administrative and technical contacts are for a domain. This will list their email address, and often their phone and FAX numbers. Whois is available via the web at:

InterNIC for US domains – http://www.internic.net/cgi-bin/whois

Ripe.net for European domains – http://www.ripe.net

▶ *Whois* – A network service that allows you to consult a database containing information about someone. A Whois query can, for example, help to find the identity of someone who is sending you unwanted email messages.

The Whois result for 209.30.124.2 tells you that no match was found. This may mean that the message is forged. The junk emailers are aware of the Whois tools as well, so don't be surprised to find false contact addresses like nobody@nowhere.com', and phone numbers that don't work. To go further, you need to find out who owns the IP address. This is likely to be the ISP or organisation that gives the spammer an internet connection. To do this you need to refer to another database which holds this information such as http://ipindex.dragonstar.net.

Searching through, we find that this particular IP address is owned by an ISP called Flash.net. There it is. Flash.net is the company which should receive your complaints: abuse@flash.net or postmaster@flash.net.

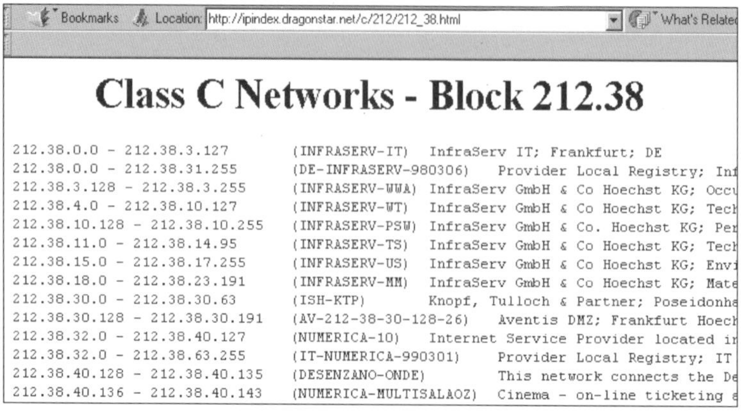

Fig. 51. If you have identified a genuine numerical IP address, you can check who owns it at the Dragonstar site. You will then have a better idea of who to complain to.

Bookmarks   Location: http://ipindex.dragonstar.net/c/212/212_38.html   What's Related

Class C Networks - Block 212.38

```
212.38.0.0 - 212.38.3.127      (INFRASERV-IT)    InfraServ IT; Frankfurt; DE
212.38.0.0 - 212.38.31.255     (DE-INFRASERV-980306)    Provider Local Registry; Inf
212.38.3.128 - 212.38.3.255    (INFRASERV-WWA) InfraServ GmbH & Co Hoechst KG; Occ
212.38.4.0 - 212.38.10.127     (INFRASERV-WT)  InfraServ GmbH & Co Hoechst KG; Tech
212.38.10.128 - 212.38.10.255  (INFRASERV-PSW) InfraServ GmbH & Co. Hoechst KG; Per
212.38.11.0 - 212.38.14.95     (INFRASERV-TS)  InfraServ GmbH & Co Hoechst KG; Tech
212.38.15.0 - 212.38.17.255    (INFRASERV-US)  InfraServ GmbH & Co Hoechst KG; Envi
212.38.18.0 - 212.38.23.191    (INFRASERV-MM)  InfraServ GmbH & Co Hoechst KG; Mate
212.38.30.0 - 212.38.30.63     (ISH-KTP)       Knopf, Tulloch & Partner; Poseidonha
212.38.30.128 - 212.38.30.191  (AV-212-38-30-128-26)    Aventis DMZ; Frankfurt Hoech
212.38.32.0 - 212.38.40.127    (NUMERICA-10)   Internet Service Provider located in
212.38.32.0 - 212.38.63.255    (IT-NUMERICA-990301)    Provider Local Registry; IT
212.38.40.128 - 212.38.40.135  (DESENZANO-ONDE)         This network connects the De
212.38.40.136 - 212.38.40.143  (NUMERICA-MULTISALAOZ)   Cinema - on-line ticketing a
```

Forged Receive' lines

Sometimes, however, some of the earlier receive' lines are also forged in an attempt to stop your complaints getting through to the correct people. Always check the numerical IP address in the square brackets ignore text and any numbers in round brackets. Finally, when you do complain, accept that the person you complain to may not be responsible and just another victim of forged emails. Be polite. For further information, go to http://samspade.org one of the best sites for combating junk mail.

Finding someone's email address

1. If you have someone's name but not their email address, you might be able to find more information in an email directory. One of the best is BigFoot (http://uk.bigfoot.com). All you need to do is enter the person's first and last name and click the Search' button. You will then be given a list of email addresses for people with that name. Try it yourself: Point your browser at Bigfoot and enter your own name. You might be surprised at how many others share your name, even if it is quite uncommon.

Fig. 52. There's a chance that you could find out more about a spammer or stalker by visiting a popular email directory like Bigfoot.

2. Yahoo! People Search is another good site (http://people.yahoo.com/). On BigFoot and the Yahoo! site, you can perform an advanced directory search. Advanced searching can fine-tune your search and reduce the number of entries returned by the search. If you know the town where that person lives, or the organisation, or node', you can narrow down the list.

3. Try Telephone Directories on the Web (http://www.teldir.com), the internet's most detailed index of online phone books. It will give you links to yellow pages, white pages, business directories, email addresses and fax listings from all over the world. Many of the entries are out of date, but you might be lucky.

4. The Ultimates (http://www.theultimates.com), developed by Scott Martin, is a handy site. With this one you can search several different reference sources by filling out one online form. The site is great for locating people or businesses because it enables you to search white

pages, yellow pages, or email directories through a common interface. You can click the Ultimates Email Directory, for example, to search six different directory services, including BigFoot, WhoWhere, and Four11. Just fill out the first form; when you tab to the next field, scripts automatically copy your entry to the corresponding fields for the other services. Once you track down an address, you can even use the Ultimate Trip Planner to find maps and routes for getting there.

5. And finally you can try WhoWhere (http://www.whowhere.lycos.com). This is operated by Lycos, one of the big search engines, and provides its service as a part of the search site as a whole. And, if you want to feed information to the lion, you can add and update your email address, add your homepage URL and include a phone number.

Deja.com and Usenet

As mentioned on page 28, Deja.com archives Usenet posts. A search for a person by name can, depending on the rarity of the name, bring up lots of information about a person, including their email address and much more. The person who is sending you the unwanted emails may have left a trail on Usenet.

Using anti-spam software

If the sender of unsolicited emails can use automated software, so can you. Spam Hater, for example, is free Windows software that helps you respond effectively. It analyses the spam, extracts a list of addresses, prepares a reply, includes a copy of the spam, and puts it in a mail window ready for sending. You have a choice of some standard legal threats, insults, or you can create your own message. At the very least, Spam Hater makes you feel less of a victim and more of a fighter.

Spam Hater can also generates a 'WHOIS' query to help track the sender and a 'traceroute' query to help track the perpetrator's provider.

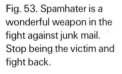

Fig. 53. Spamhater is a wonderful weapon in the fight against junk mail. Stop being the victim and fight back.

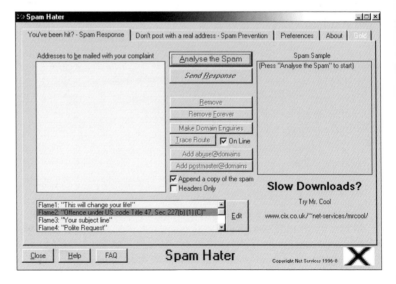

You simply view the spam in your email program, select 'Analyse the spam', Check the list of addresses for errors, and click on 'Send response'. Spam Hater will open a new mail and fill in the address, subject and message content. You then just send it off in the normal way. Spam Hater can also be used for posting to Usenet with an anonymous address to foil address collection software used by spammers.

If you use Outlook Express, you must perform the following sequence before analysing the spam:

1. Click File and then Properties.
2. Click the Details tab.
3. Click the Message Source button.

To download SpamHater: http://www.compulink.co.uk/~net-services/spam/
For other anti-spam software: http://ftp.cura.net/spam95.html
Or try ZDNet: http://www.hotfiles.com/roundups/spam/rnp0897.html.

Using encryption

'Past wars have been won or lost because the most powerful governments on earth didn't have the cryptological power any interested junior high school student with a personal computer can harness today. Soon any child old enough to use a computer will be able to transmit encoded messages that no government on earth will find easy to decipher.' *Bill Gates.*

The morality of secrecy
Secrecy has become a habit for all of us. After all, most of us use passwords, PIN numbers or keys to get us something or somewhere that other people are denied access to. The oldest known example of a lock and key came from the ruins of the palace of Khorsabad near Nineveh in the Near East, and dates from around 4,000 years ago.

Since then and before, we have been obsessed with privacy. What has been behind our closed doors has been guarded jealously. Today, your computer files and internet messages will often contain information that you do not want anyone you do not trust to read.

Keeping messages secret does not mean that you are a criminal. On the contrary, it is the criminal who has most to gain from reading your messages. Sending credit card details or other personal details by email, for instance, is a risky business. An email message is often saved on several different computers on its rapid flight across the internet. At any one of those points, the information in the message is vulnerable.

Simple encryption
Most forms of encryption are based on a key of some kind. One of the simplest codes used on the internet is ROTT 13, which is sometimes used to keep unsuitable messages from being read by young children. With ROTT 13, the letters in a message are substituted for the one thirteen places after it. In other words, A is substituted by N, B is substituted by O, and so on. The message 'Kye's birthday present is

under the bed' becomes 'Xlr'f oveguqnl cerfrag vf haqre gur orq'. However, only the youngest cybersnoop would be fooled by this simple encryption.

PGP: strong encryption

ROTT 13 is obviously very limited and would not deter even a young child for long; for more sensitive information such as credit card details you clearly would need a form of encryption that is far more difficult to crack. Probably the best publicly available system is Pretty Good Privacy or PGP. A member of The Guild (a hacker group) wrote about the difficulty of breaking a message encoded with PGP. 'If you had 1,000,000,000 machines that could try 1,000,000,000 keys per second, it would still take all these machines longer than the universe as we know it has existed and then some, to find the key.'

An organisation with access to powerful supercomputers, such as a government intelligence agency, might crack your public key by using a secret breakthrough. (With the existence of 'moles' it might be difficult to keep the breakthrough secret.) Civilian experts have been trying to break public key cryptography since 1978 without success.

▶ *PGP* – Pretty Good Privacy is probably the strongest method of encryption publicly available.

PGP is such a good system that some countries such as USA, Canada and Japan classify it as a weapon. They have tried to make it as difficult to export some forms of PGP as it is to export grenades or ground-to-air missiles. Phil Zimmerman, the creator of the PGP system, completed PGP just as rumours were coming from Washington that strong encryption could soon be outlawed completely. Realising that PGP would be included, he released the source code free of charge. Friends of his also published the code on the internet, making it available to the whole world overnight. Zimmerman was put under investigation by the FBI for 'illegal arms trafficking'. In releasing PGP on the internet, he gave the ordinary person in the street the ability to send

Fig. 54. The international home page of PGP ('Pretty Good Privacy') tells you where to obtain full strength encryption without coming up against local US exportation laws. For encrypting your emails, PGP is probably the most secure method.

messages that could stay private even when under attack by the best intelligence services. Whether he is a hero or an anarchist, future histories books will show.

So how does PGP work? ROTT 13 uses a key (13) to encrypt a message; everyone (except the young children it is meant to protect) knows the key: it is a public key. PGP also uses public keys, but both the keys and the way they are used are far more complex. And PGP uses not only the public key but needs a second, private, key. These two complementary keys – a 'key pair' – are used together to encrypt a message. If you use PGP, you must first create a key pair before you can begin exchanging encrypted email with other PGP users.

To send someone a PGP-encrypted email message, you use a copy of that person's public key to encrypt the message. They then unlock it with their private key. When someone sends you an encrypted message, they use a copy of your public key to encrypt the data, and only you can unlock the message by using your private key.

It can be explained more simply by comparing your public key with a set of identical padlocks (the public keys). You own a set of brand new, high quality padlocks. You give each of your friends and business associates one of these padlocks. When they send you a box of goodies, they first lock it using your padlock. Once the box is closed, the box can only be opened with your key (private key). Giving your public key away is not a risk to you: the padlock itself is useless to anybody unless they are sending something to you, because only you can open the padlock once it is closed.

Once a person has a copy of your public key – unlike a padlock which has to be sent back to them each time – they can use it over and over again whenever they want to send a PGP message to you. Public keys are simply blocks of text so you can send it by ordinary email (see below).

An example of a public key (PGP freeware version 6.0.21)

mQGIBDbrRZERBADzuw1Fw1f1ddbeujSZDAP19fsKCz+QFgsh
DLMOVd+LNkPoB9aOh6wQKX4WK1/7oWMZ3FLAO1NjXcb
qW7Uva9fbQzdpTo1pG7uJNgw+CED55zd6QOYJBYDCWy0fx
BFf7GGrSzxwZdJk49WnyeNYOgjt2rBrGNcTqDPaENh3U3j2
PwCg/+PVZX9x2Uk89PY3bzpnhV5JZzf24rnRPxfx2vIPFRzB
hznzJZv8VDS2nyOFQI+jqyIDmmWAz8JTPFdtdwDIdMc2rpQ
71FQhSlpKDyBpNPKQoDE3mv9PEhKPbw7Bze+hTSYCX6Ru
RJfoWOFLNEI7qkusRGEnqJ9XTEfEeGCJ6Z2vhXV52xChY42
6zJCHHHUa5N/fGHh2ar0eINRRVOsTmEIuEfGzAcjRYEdqYAu
AsBqybpLZcpqXyaJpKZbdRmWrrvKuzjBabz/bq4Ib7geU/dCs
u2cOrPUS2TsvFU/7bxLm95Y+RaUI4IekhzCx1UB4ZOIbvTIZIz
oRIF4D2fQIQBGBBgRAgAGBQI260WRAAoJEB0A3sIK2Yc8x
RoAoLExr+t4UZVLg4ISzbnGn4JHt1YzAJ4rNdYZQFnanwzfR
HJWR7nevc+hgw===u43A

Public keys can also be made 'public' in a more literal sense by publishing them on the internet on 'key servers'. If someone wants to send you a secure message but does not have your public key, they can get a copy from a key server.

▶ *Key server* – A computer on the internet that exists to store people's public PGP keys. If you do not encrypt your internet communications, it is a simple matter for an attacker to intercept your messages, especially email. If you use PGP sensibly, the attacker will have to expend far more effort and expense to achieve the same access to your information.

Some essential precautions to take that will ensure that your keys are secure:

1. If someone breaks into your house, all of your efforts with PGP will come to nothing if your passphrases or keys are easily accessible. Don't leave either on a scrap of paper or in a plain text file on your computer. This is also important if you are using a computer at work or on a shared computer.

2. Just because you use PGP, don't feel that you are invulnerable. Cryptography can only protect data while it's encrypted – if someone steals or gains access to your computer, they can still obtain unencrypted information.

▶ *Passphrase* – This is a phrase like a password but more secure because it uses more letters and is more difficult to guess or work out.

PGP is not designed to protect your data while it is in plaintext form on a compromised system. Nor can it prevent an intruder from using sophisticated measures to read your private key while it is being used. You will just have to recognise these risks on multi-user systems, and adjust your expectations and behaviour accordingly. Perhaps your situation is such that you should consider only running PGP on an isolated single-user system under your direct physical control.

The length of your keys is also a factor. Keys are basically very big numbers. Key size is measured in bits; the number representing a 1024-bit key is huge. In public key cryptography, the bigger the key, the more secure the encoded message. A key length of 40 bits is poor security, but 1024 bits would keep out the most persistent attacker.

What governments think
PGP is at the forefront of a new war between private users and governments. Many governments dislike the idea of private citizens and businesses using PGP, unless they turn over their private keys to the government. PGP can protect the privacy of normal users as well as criminals, but the truth is that encryption such as PGP is only giving the user the level of privacy on the internet that normal letters have always had.

'Researchers demonstrate computer code can be broken. Researchers this week proved that 512-bit encryption, the standard used to protect

most online financial transactions, is not secure. The international group of researchers broke the security codes in seven months and required 292 computers at 11 different sites. However, one participating researcher says the codes could be broken in less than a week using the computing power of government agencies or large enterprises. By demonstrating the inadequacy of 512-bit encryption, the researchers have also fuelled doubts about U.S. export control laws regulating encryption. Currently, 512 bits is the strongest level of encryption that can be exported in most instances.'
(*The New York Times*, 27th August 1999).

Using digital signatures

At the other end of the privacy scale is the need to prove to others that a message is actually from you, and not forged. Normal documents are verified by the use of a hand-written signature. Electronic documents can be signed with an electronic signature or certificate.

▶ *Digital signature* – A way of including your identity in a message that uses encryption so that the message would be extremely difficult to forge.

Online shopping and electronic banking are becoming more commonplace but relatively few people trust the internet enough to use it for payments of any kind. Online payment offers the convenience and flexibility of 24-hour service from home. Encryption alone is not seen as enough because it does not prove that you, or the store, are genuinely who you say you are. Digital signatures provide the solution. They provide a means of verifying someone's identity electronically.

Besides being an excellent method of encryption, PGP can also be used to digitally sign your messages and other online transactions. Normally, when you send a plain message to someone, anyone intercepting that message can change it and let it continue on its way as if nothing had happened.

Suppose you sent a request to transfer £10 to someone's account. If the message was intercepted and changed to read £100, you might not be aware for months that anything was wrong. Or if a friendly message was changed to a more hostile tone, you could end up in court. One way to prevent this kind of tampering is to send information about the message itself in a 'digital signature' – a simple example could be the number of characters in the message. When you receive a message, you can check the actual message length in characters with the information in the digital signature. Of course, the information can be changed at the same time to agree with the changed message.

In a PGP signature, this extra information is calculated in a far more complicated way than simply adding the number of characters in the message and it is locked so that nobody can change it without the signature becoming invalid. When you sends someone a digitally signed message, the recipient can use the hidden information in the signature to check that the plain text of the message has not been altered in any way and that it was sent by you. The recipients use their copy of your public key to determine if you really sent the email and whether it has been altered while in transit. The process is similar to recognising someone's hand-written signature on a cheque but uses some complex mathematics to verify that the digital signature is genuine.

Additional benefits of digital signatures
Additional benefits to the use of a digital signature are that it can easily be sent to others, cannot be easily repudiated or imitated by someone else, and can contain information about when the message was sent. A digital signature can be used with any kind of message, whether it is encrypted or not, simply so that the receiver can be sure of the sender's identity and that the message arrived intact.

Using digital certificates
A digital certificate, or site certificate, is a kind of signature or electronic credential. It is used when doing business on the web. Certificates are usually checked by your browser and issued by a certification authority (CA) such as RSA, Verisign or Thawte. The certificate will contain information such as:

1. your public key
2. your name
3. the expiry date of the public key
4. the name of the issuer
5. serial number of the certificate
6. the digital signature of the issuer

Digital certificates can be seen as the electronic equivalent of a passport, or driving licence. Your digital certificate electronically proves your identity, or your right to access information or services online. Your identity is coded into a pair of electronic keys, as in PGP encryption, which can be used to encrypt and digitally sign information. A certificate helps to stop people using forged keys to impersonate others. Used in combination with encryption, certificates provide far stronger security, and for all practical purposes guarantee the identities of the parties to a transaction.

If you receive a certificated message, you decrypt it – if necessary using the sender's public key. You verify that it is from the real sender by checking the digital signature of the issuing authority. Digital certificates are often kept in online registries so authenticated users can look up other people's public keys.

Site certificates are simply another name for digital certificates used to verify secure servers such as online shops or banks. Secure web sites have the prefix https instead of http. When you connect to a secure server, your browser checks its certificate and warns you if it cannot verify it.

Fig. 55. The Thawte 'web of trust' has established itself as the most trusted and respected certificate-issuing authority on the internet.

The Thawte Web of Trust system

The method considered to be safest by many is the Thawte web of trust. At present it is the only certificate-issuing agency to support the powerful encryption that PGP allows outside the USA. For this reason Thawte is the only realistic and secure certificate system for countries outside the USA. Personal certificates are free and verify you as an individual.

Personal certificates are the best technology available to perform secure authentication on the internet. They combine the ease of use of password-based access with the security of PGP encryption. You can use personal certificates to create secure communications between friends and business partners across the internet. Thawte verifies your identity by requiring you to make a personal visit to a minimum of three recognised notaries to produce documents such as driver's license, military IDs and passports. The notaries verify and copy the documents and send completed paperwork to Thawte. Thawte then validates the certification and you, or the certified user, are notified by email of the certification, and then you can download and register your certificate.

Thus your certificate is proof of your identity and their certificate guarantees that they have been positively identified. Because of the dangers of forged web sites and other cons on the web, the 'web of trust' from Thawte is the best means of your protecting yourself and your identity on the web.

Maintaining privacy at work

There is little you can really do to keep your internet activities private at work. Your employer practically owns you and everything on your computer while you are at work. If you are linked in to a company network, your use of the computer will be automatically logged in great detail. If you use a company laptop at home, the company can probably lay claim to anything you do on it at home.

Always assume there is no such thing as private email when you are using a company computer. Always assume that all of your actions on the internet are being logged. There are some precautions you can take, however:

Protecting your privacy . . . .

1. Don't use the web for anything other than work-related business.

2. Don't put anything in an email that you would not want any of the following to see: your boss, a solicitor, a judge, the police, the taxman, your colleagues, a competing company – in short, anybody apart from the person you intend to send it to.

3. Remember that when you 'delete' an email message or file, it will probably remain stored on the company's central computer system, or in a backup store, for a very long time.

4. Don't assume that just because you send an email to a trusted friend, other less friendly people will not read it. The recipient of a message may not be as careful with information as you are, or may not be as friendly as you had assumed.

5. Think before you get angry by email. Don't open yourself to prosecution just because of a thoughtless or rash remark. The same applies to talking about your company – don't discuss sensitive company information.

6. Treat your computer passwords like your house keys. Don't make them simple, don't leave them lying around (on bits of paper etc), and change them occasionally.

7. Be as discreet as you would be when having a discussion in a busy restaurant, where you can be seen by many people and overheard by some of them.

6 Staying anonymous on the web

In this chapter we will explore:

▶ *the case for a right to anonymity*

▶ *anonymous email*

▶ *using remailers*

▶ *using web-based anonymous email*

▶ *anonymous surfing*

▶ *case studies*

. . . .

The case for a right to anonymity

Your online activities are more or less an open book, but there are some very effective tools that will enable you to become anonymous – to hide your real identity. The people who greedily build profiles of us question the need for anonymity. They try to accuse us by saying, 'What have you to hide?' In that case, should we object the police having our front door key and entering our homes at any time? Should we object to government agencies reading and copying every letter we post, or listening in to every phone call we make?

Before we sit back and let governments legislate away our human rights to privacy, let's step back a moment and consider. There are many legitimate reasons why someone might need to communicate anonymously without criminal intent. What if your employer routinely dumps chemicals in the local river, or your boss routinely sexually harasses a colleague? What if your family includes a homosexual facing intimidation, or someone who posts evidence on the web about police racism or corruption? What if there are personal and sensitive health or legal matters you want to enquire about anonymously?

All over the world, innocent people are routinely persecuted and discriminated against if identified. In today's world of ever more draconian regulation, you, a close friend or member of your family could very easily become one of them. Silence, apathy and fear open the way to dictatorial government. No matter how open you are, there will be times when you become aware of an injustice, but remain silent for fear of the consequences unless you can communicate anonymously.

The services described here will enable you to pass information without direct retribution. For example, 'whistleblowers' reporting on repressive government abuses can bring issues to light without the fear of retaliation. Employees will be able to report cases of pollution, illegal exports or falsified records without losing their jobs. Torture victims of someone like General Pinochet in Chile can report their experiences. Human rights activists in Kosovo, Chechnya – or even London – can spread the word about violations of civil liberties.

British police forces run telephone services that allow anonymous reporting of crimes. Shouldn't the internet be available in the same way? It is a perfect medium for a person to give anonymous tip-offs. Phone conversations can be overheard or tapped easily by anyone with a little equipment, but some anonymous online services are extremely difficult even for the most dictatorial governments to eavesdrop on.

Anonymity can give a desperate person the confidence to ask for advice or help, where otherwise they would not step forward for fear of embarrassment or worse. Sensitive or personal information is often posted to Usenet groups – anonymity can make this safe. On the other hand, the use of these services can make it easy for criminals to communicate in secret and hard for government agencies to enforce laws. The inability to trace the source and content of a message may stop the police convicting criminals like terrorists, paedophiles, and drug dealers.

A new US police report says that anonymity is breeding a new type of obsessive who uses the internet to destroy victims' lives. One case is that of a Hollywood security guard who became obsessed with a woman. When he was rejected, he found revenge on Usenet. He pretended to be a young woman with sado-masochistic rape fantasies and entered the woman's address as his own. As a result, her house was broken into by men, evidently seeking some sadistic entertainment. The security guard was tracked down and sentenced to six years in prison.

The verdict?

It is impossible to judge whether anonymous services do more harm than good. By their very nature, they are anonymous. If anonymous services were taken away, the technically minded criminal would quickly recover, but what alternative would there be for ordinary people who feared persecution or discrimination?

The Register[1] says that: 'The non-accountability of the internet is an ideal breeding ground for the darker elements of society. Let's hope the authorities manage to keep up with evolving technology.' The authorities may not be able to catch up, never mind keep up. So it would seem

Fig. 56. Cyberstalking is a growing crime on the internet. Stalkers think they can manipulate others more easily on the internet. Indeed they can, unless the intended victims use the 'cyber defence' tools and methods that are now available.

1. http://www.theregister.co.uk/991129-000023.html

sensible to educate potential victims and allow them to become anonymous to protect themselves, instead of letting them remain vulnerable to cyber stalkers and other criminals.

Criminals use encryption, but they also use fast cars, gloves, stockings, and the postal service. So, should fast cars, gloves, stockings and the postal service be outlawed? Surely not. Just as your homes should have locks capable of keeping even the most determined people out, so internet users should be entitled to remain anonymous to protect themselves. Just because a padlock may hinder a police for search for drugs is no reason to confiscate all padlocks, or demand all keys. Privacy stops more criminal activity – including oppression and persecution – than banning anonymity would.

Tightening up on all personal anonymity would be massively opposed by large corporations not wanting their communications to become open. Even if all opposition were to be overcome, every country in the world would have to adopt new laws, because wherever an anonymous service exists, it can be used by anyone on the internet.

In 1995 Britain's technology minister, Ian Taylor, admitted that it is virtually impossible for a government to dictate what can be done on the internet.[2] Chris Smith, the Labour MP, said: 'There are clear benefits to remailers [see below], for support groups and so on, but also dangers in that criminal activities could be undertaken. I'm not sure there is any system that can preserve the benefits but avoid the downside.'[3]

Using anonymous email

Let's say you are a clerk or a manager working for a large company and you realise that there are irregularities in some of the safety claims. You discover that the cause of a recent chemical spillage has been falsified. You know that if you inform the authorities by email, you will probably be found out and lose your job or worse. What do you do? Or suppose you are a student in a third-world dictatorship who wants to tell the rest of the world where there are torture victims. Several other students have 'disappeared' after having talked to the media. How do you get the word out without being identified?

▶ Do you think there should be a crackdown on privacy rights in your own country, but increased privacy rights for dissidents overseas?

Normally it is very easy to find the identity of the sender of an email message or a Usenet post far easier than it is for a normal letter. The header of an email message contains information that can identify you to others (see page 99 for examples of headers). The header also contains information about the route that the message took through the internet. So how do you make your email anonymous? With snail mail, you can simply omit your return address. If you want a reply, you can use a PO box number for replies.

2. *New Scientist*, 27 February 1995.
3. *New Scientist*, 11 March 1995.

Staying anonymous on the web ....

With email, you must use an anonymous remailer, which will deal with sending and receiving email. Anonymous mailing services preserve your privacy by acting as a go-between when you browse the web or send messages. Such services slow your internet experience, but if you need anonymity any time, that is a very small price to pay.

Using remailers

An anonymous remailer is a computer service that allows you to send an email message or Usenet post without revealing your identity to anyone who reads or intercepts the message, including the recipient if need be. Some remailers also permit you to send email while protecting your email records from your internet Service Provider. There are basically three types of remailers: pseudo-anonymous, cypherpunk and mixmasters.

1. Pseudo-anonymous remailers

Say you work for a company called Gooey Chemicals and have a friend in a similar company called Sticky Chemicals. To discuss the extent of chemical spillage by your employers before reporting them to the authorities, you might use a remailer that would strip the real name and address off your message and replace it with dummy information and forward the message on to the recipient. If your friend replies to the message, the remailer will similarly strip out the name of the person replying, thus protecting everyone's privacy. Nobody is sacked.

The above is an example of a pseudo anonymous remailer. You open an account with an operator and trust that he does not reveal your identity, the content of your messages or their destinations.

This example contains weaknesses, though. Messages can be tracked going in and coming out of the remailer. If only one remailer is used, the remailer operator knows both the originating and final addresses and, unless the message is encrypted, the content of the message. Your company could track your messages up to the remailer and track outgoing messages which coincide with your message. Even though the identities may have changed, the size of the message will not. If they intercept the message which comes out of the remailer after yours goes in, your employer might be able to track your message and discover the recipient.

Alternatively, the company could try to pressure the remailer operator to divulge the information. There have been many occasions where a government has forced a remailer operator to hand over information about one of its users (so much for privacy policies). It is possible that a powerful company could do the same. Truly anonymous remailers are far more secure than pseudo-anonymous remailers, but they are also much harder to use. The next step up in security is the Cypherpunk remailer.

2. Cypherpunk remailers

To understand how Cypherpunk remailers send messages, consider sending a parcel secretly to someone. The wrapping paper is the encryption and the enclosed present is the message. Let's use two remailers for simplicity.

You wrap the parcel up in three layers of paper. Each layer contains the address of the next person to post it to. So first, you (the message sender) would wrap up your present. Each layer has on it a label with a person's name and the outer layer also has your return address.

You 'send' the wrapped (encrypted) message to the first person, John (first remailer). John takes a layer of paper off and puts it in a file; he reads the name of the next person, Jane (second remailer), and delivers it to her after adding his return address to the new wrapping. Jane receives the parcel and knows it is from John, but she does not know that you are the original sender because John has removed the wrapper with your address (email header information). Jane now removes the next layer of paper, puts it to one side and reads the name of the recipient of the parcel (Jackie) and delivers it to her after adding her own return address to the wrapper. Jackie now removes the final layer and opens the present (a box of chocolate from a secret admirer).

Now, Jackie can reply to the admirer even though she does not know his identity because she sends it to Jane's return address; Jane then sends it to John who sends it to you. Each person who handles the parcel, apart from you and the recipient, is a remailer.

So Cypherpunk remailers send messages wrapped in a number of encrypted layers. Each remailer in the link removes a layer of encryption and follows the next set of instructions to send the message on to the next destination. Each remailer knows only the identity of the immediate links in the chain.

If you want maximum privacy, you should send your message through two or more remailers. If done properly, you can ensure that *nobody* (no remailer operator or any snoop) can read both your real name and your message. This is the real meaning of anonymous. In practice, nobody can force an anonymous remailer operator to reveal your identity, because the operator has *no clue* who you are. There is a slight possibility that two remailer operators will collaborate and reveal your identity, but using

Fig. 57. Zedz Consultants offer a range of tools for people and organisations wishing to remain anonymous. These tools include using a remailer and encryption. The site is under development, so it is worth checking back to see what is new.

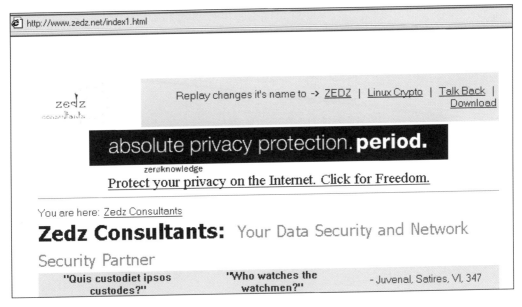

three or more links in the chain makes it a truly awesome task to try to identify both the sender and recipient.

Sending an encrypted message through a chain of remailers is extremely secure but messages can still be traced through the chain because the remailers often forward a message straightaway. The tracked message arrives and another leaves soon after – presumably the same message with a different header and level of encryption. Anyone monitoring might rightly assume that it is the same message. They then track the second message to the next link in the chain. This may also be done long after the messages have been relayed if the remailer has logged the emails.

One way of tracing messages through a chain of remailers is to capture a single message and send lots of identical copies of it to the remailer. The remailer will then send lots of identical messages to the next destination. Anyone tracking these messages will be able to identify the route and destination of the message. The process can then be repeated each link in the chain. Another class of remailer, the Mixmaster, overcomes some of the weaknesses of Cypherpunk remailers.

3. Mixmasters

The Mixmaster remailing system relies on a special message format. All messages are identical in size (or broken up into identically sized packets). The message format also contains information that stops an attacker replaying copies of a message. Each packet contains 20 headers. Each time a header is stripped, the packet is bulked up again with random junk to the correct size.

Using Mixmaster remailers is fairly complex at present and beyond the needs of all but those in extremely sensitive situations. More information can be found at:

http://obscura.com/~loki/index.cgi

Fig. 58. Mixmaster remailers are complex to understand and use, but the security they offer will challenge even the most resourceful attackers, including government surveillance agencies.

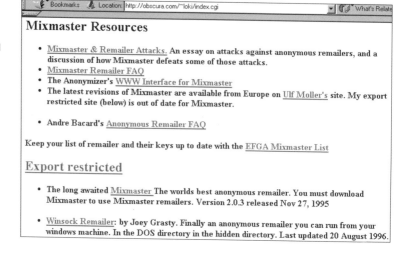

Using web-based anonymous email

Hushmail
http://www.hushmail.com

One of the great new developments on the internet has been web-based email services like Hotmail, Yahoo! mail, and Excite mail. The advantage is that you can have an international email address that you can access from anywhere in the world without needing your own ISP access. You can use a computer belonging to a friend, or log on at an internet café. Now the idea has gone one step further with the introduction of an encrypted web-based email service: HushMail.

Hushmail uses 1024-bit encryption. The log-on process creates your key by taking information from your mouse as you move it around. Your choice of password controls how secure your mailings are. In other words, the more difficult your password is to crack (read how to make a secure password on page 72), the more secure your messages. Hush-Mail uses java applets to encrypt your web-based email with public-key encryption and claims to be the world's first 'fully encrypted, truly secure, free web-based email client.'

▶ *Email client* – Another term for your email program (Outlook, Messenger, Eudora etc).

▶ *Web client* – Another term for your web browser (Internet Explorer, Netscape, Oracle etc).

The main drawback is that the person you're emailing also needs to have a HushMail account in order to decode your message. There are also slight risks from the use of Java and the fact that you have to trust one company, unlike a chain of anonymous remailers. For people who want good security and need the ability to send and receive email from anywhere, such as journalists, HushMail is great.

Signing on to use HushMail is simple: just click on 'Create an account' and you'll be asked for a username and some other information. Move

Fig. 59. A convenient way to ensure secure email while roaming the planet is Hushmail. Since it is web-based, you can use it anywhere, such as at a cybercafé or college.

your mouse around to generate a random set of keys and you're ready to send secure email. You don't need any special software or complicated configuration. You can register in less than two minutes. HushMail uses a process called 'public key cryptosystem with roaming user capability.' The only people who can read your mail are the people that you send it to. It also means that you can access your account from any computer which has a web browser and internet access, anywhere in the world.

ZipLip
http://www.ZipLip.com
ZipLip is a web-based email service rather like HushMail. Your message is stored in encrypted format at the site itself. ZipLip then notifies your recipient that your message is waiting for them. In turn, your recipient goes to ZipLip and picks up the message. After it has been read, all traces of the message are removed. ZipLip uses encryption techniques based on Verisign certificates. However, the problem of exporting encryption products does not arise because the message never leaves their server. If you protect your mail with a password, your message and the password is stored in an encrypted format which not even ZipLip can read. Your message is decrypted only when the recipient supplies the correct password. There is no registration or information to give away about yourself.

Fig. 60. If you send an encrypted message to ZipLip, it will remain there until the recipient picks it up. Not even ZipLip can read it.

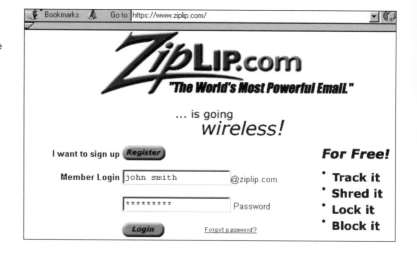

Anonymous surfing

Anonymizer
http://www.anonymizer.com
Anonymizer lets you know just how much information you are giving away when you browse the web. Even if you have no plans to browse anonymously, it is well worth visiting the site to see what information it has about you. Once you have recovered from the shock, it allows you to surf anonymously. Sending email also puts information in the hands of anybody who cares to look. The company claims to be the most secure

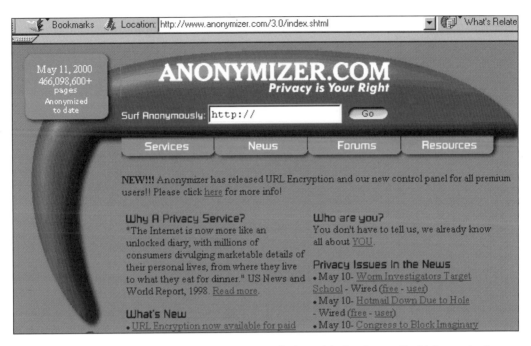

way in the world, apart from the military, to use email. Just visit the site, type your message and let Anonymizer send it securely.

Rewebber
http://www.rewebber.de

The Rewebber is a service that 'guarantees anonymity for WWW clients' (browsers) and servers by removing information about the user. Then the request is forwarded to the web site whose response is then forwarded back to you through Rewebber. Rewebber exists as a go-between so that you don't need to give away information in order to view a site. Rewebber is funded by advertising, so to insert the ads they use Java-Script. The Rewebber removes all the JavaScript tags it receives from

Fig. 61. Anonymizer is one of the best-known and longest-running privacy sites. It offers a reliable and private way to use the internet.

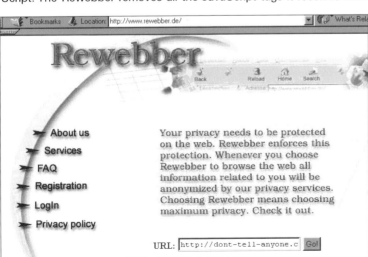

Fig. 62. Rewebber is another long-standing anonymous service, and well known to anyone who has learned how to defend their privacy.

other servers, but since there is no other technique it inserts some Java-Script to help with placing ads in a separate frame. There is no risk in enabling JavaScript if you view all sites through the Rewebber. This is because all JavaScript commands come directly from the Rewebber itself. Alternatively, if you have Internet Explorer 5, you can add Rewebber to your 'Trusted Sites' list.

Nym
http://www.publius.net/n.a.n.help.html
Nym allows the creation of a set of pseudonyms that you can use in combination with PGP encryption to give 'the highest degree of privacy possible'. This requires a great deal of complexity in the message formats, so to use Nym you should download special software[4] that will handle the details for you. The complexity of the Nym system is beyond the scope of this book but further details can be obtained at the Nym.alias.net site mentioned above.

Fig. 63. Nym allows you to set up and use an alternative identity ('nym') on the internet. This way your real personal information remains (as it should) your private property.

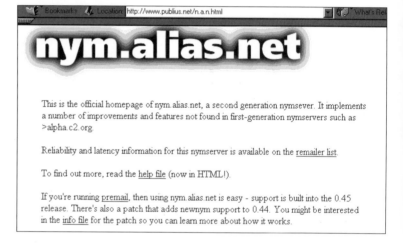

Freedom
http://www.zeroknowledge.com
Another service that uses pseudonyms is Zero Knowledge Systems (ZKS). ZKS is a Canadian company that sells a software package called Freedom. This package allows people to use the internet while remaining anonymous. The system works by a combination of encryption and pseudonyms that are wrapped around the user's email messages so that the content and the sender remain private. Freedom also takes control of the 'cookies' that many web sites leave on your hard disk.

Freedom lets you use up to five pseudonyms or nyms (personal digital identities) when you browse the web. Each nym is represented by an email address ending in freedom.net, e.g. mark@freedom.net and jane@freedom.net. As you browse the web using a nym, it will begin to collect its own cookies, reputation, and history, but as soon as you switch to a different nym, you're a completely different person as far as

4. Such as Jack Be Nimble from http://www.members.tripod.com/ ~14795/jbn/

Fig. 64. The Canadian company Zero Knowledge Systems (ZKS) has recently developed some powerful privacy software called Freedom. It has been deluged with enquiries from Americans worried about the rise in US government eavesdropping; they would rather trust a Canadian solution.

anyone can tell. Not only will people be unable to identify you from the nym, they won't be able to relate nyms with one another. In fact not even Zero Knowledge themselves will be able to tell who is behind a given pseudonym.

Internet communications usually travel unencrypted and pass through servers that can be easily identified. This is like sending a postcard – anyone handling it can read it and see the address of the recipient and sender. Interception, forgery and tracking is made easy with this kind of communication. Freedom software ensures that each server in the chain knows only the previous and following servers in the journey from source to destination. The servers know nothing about the content of the communication. No single server knows both the origin and the destination of the traffic. Not even your ISP can then monitor your web activities.

Case study

In November 1999 Frank Lu, a human rights monitor, was working in Hong Kong. He reported that in the middle of a nationwide crackdown in China against dissidents, a group called Falun Gong used email to organise a secret press conference in Beijing to tell the world about police beatings of detained Falun Gong members. In response, the Chinese government recruited a large number of computer graduates to increase its monitoring of internet users' activities. 'The internet is a revolutionary tool for people's freedom,' says Lu, 'China alone can't stop this global trend.'

The Chinese government amended their criminal law in 1998 to include new 'computer crimes' such as sending email to pro-democracy groups or activists abroad. Anonymous services such as the ones mentioned in this chapter could keep thousands of human rights activists and political dissidents from being imprisoned in China, and in many other countries. They are struggling for the rights we often take for granted and could easily lose.

7 Protecting children

In this chapter we will explore:

▶ *a strategy of protection*
▶ *filtering software*
▶ *rating systems*
▶ *parental control*
▶ *tips for the kids*
▶ *government control*
▶ *Truste system*
▶ *case studies*

If your child has a computer in its room, it stops being merely a computer as soon as it is connected to the internet. It then becomes a doorway that practically anyone in the world can use to access your home via your child's bedroom. Would you like a stranger to access your child's bedroom without your knowledge?

If you are using the internet at home, you probably have uncensored and unfiltered access. If you do, you will inevitably come across people and web sites on the net which you would not want your children to come in contact with. Indeed, some would shock even the most liberal-minded adult.

A strategy of protection

There are three main ways you can protect your children:

1. Install blocking software on your computer. This gives access to the web, but it will monitor the connection and filter out any sites containing keywords marked as undesirable.
2. Enable the ratings system in your browser. The ratings system uses information about the content of a site to decide whether it is acceptable or not. The unacceptable sites are filtered out.
3. Parental guidance and education. For example, only allow the use of the computer in a communal area such as the kitchen or sitting room where people are likely to be near or pass by regularly.

Blocking software and the rating systems are forms of censorship. As adults, many of us object strongly to being censored by others. It might be possible that the internet is the only place a child can find information, advice and support. Children who have become drug users, or who may be gay, or have problems of some other kind, will find the support they need on the internet. Many of the filtering systems will unfortunately deny them access to these important sites.

By censoring your child's internet access you could be boxing the child into a corner. The decision is yours, of course, but if you opt for filtering software or a rating system, that software or system will determine what is suitable or not for your children. The list will include many sites that you might find perfectly normal or useful. Some systems have even listed sites that have criticised them for no other reason than to prevent the criticisms 'getting out'.

Of course, the above may not be relevant anyway. Many children know already how to crack the software so that they can bypass its filters. And once one child has cracked the software, the know-how will spread to children all over the world. See for yourself by visiting the remarkable Peacefire site, set up by an American teenager:

http://www.peacefire.org

If you insist on installing filtering software, read on.

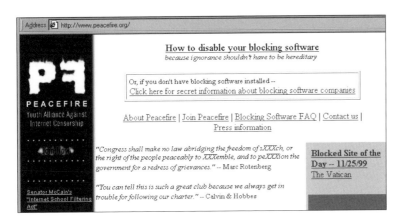

Fig. 65. Teenagers are fighting against censorship by adults. They have formed online groups like Peacefire to support one another and develop solutions suitable for their age group and culture.

Filtering software

Netnanny
http://www.netnanny.com
Net Nanny blocks or screens unsuitable material and also prevents your address, phone and credit card numbers from being given out on the internet. Net Nanny is capable of monitoring the web, email, chat programs, newsgroups and offline applications. It gives you as parent, guardian or teacher, control over what is being accessed. They claim, 'Net Nanny gives the parent or administrator complete control over what is being accessed.' It's up to you to determine the levels of access, and areas of access for each user. You can allow full access, or deny access altogether. You determine the levels of access, and areas of access for each user.

Net Nanny uses lists of web sites that are free and can be updated automatically within the program. You can also set up your own lists. You can block specific words, phrases, web sites, chat rooms, newsgroups and personal information. You can set the program to block transmission of children's names and ages, home addresses, telephone

Fig. 66. The NetNanny logo.

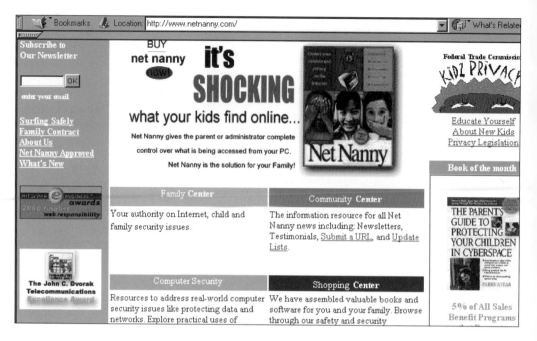

numbers, credit card numbers and social insurance numbers. The idea is to stop your children giving away sensitive information out of innocence.

You can set Net Nanny to react to violations in a variety of ways, including a warning, masking words or phrase, logging the violation, or shutting down the application. In addition, the warning message can be edited so it is different for each user. Net Nanny costs $26.95 but a 30- day demo can be downloaded from the site.

SurfMonkey

http://www.surfmonkey.com

Perhaps the best kind of blocking software is both unobtrusive and fun. Yes, such a thing does exist! SurfMonkey is a browser based on Internet Explorer but designed to be user-friendly to younger children. There is a helper: a monkey that pops up to offer advice and tips. The main screen of SurfMonkey has the appearance of the inside of a space ship with simple navigation buttons on the console. As with all good cartoon spaceships, there are also some simple 'weapons'. This has a bomb but-

ton which 'explodes' the web page being viewed, and a splat button, which throws coloured blobs onto it.

There are, of course, various filtering options. Before a site is visited, it is checked against a blacklist of hundreds of thousands of sites. It also blocks communication with strangers and 5,000 news groups. Updates to the approved and blocked lists are made automatically each time the child queries a web site.

The Surf Monkey site also serves as a portal, allowing access to many safe and fun resources for children. The site is designed to allow access to appropriate sites and prevent access to inappropriate sites. Their Kids' Channel web site has monitored chat rooms. This, combined with a large number of pre-stored sites, makes SurfMonkey a worthwhile browser.

The browser is a large program to download but there is a navigation bar that will take a couple of minutes to download and, for a little more time, you can opt to download the animated monkey character.

The Surf Monkey Bar sits at the bottom of Internet Explorer window and has a password-protected toggle switch so you can turn the bar on or off.

CyberSitter
http://www.pow-dist.co.uk
CyberSitter is Windows 95 program that can block access to common types of graphic files and other files and programs. You can set the software to block the file or sound an alarm when your child tries to access them. CyberSitter says: 'Working secretly in the background, CyberSitter analyses all internet activity. Whenever it detects activity the parent has elected to restrict, it takes over and blocks the activity before it takes place. If desired, CyberSitter will maintain a complete history of all internet activity, including attempts to access blocked material.'

Fig. 69. Cybersitter is another filter for children. This one can also act as a spy on the computer, watching and recording everything that the user of that computer – child or anyone else – does while on the internet.

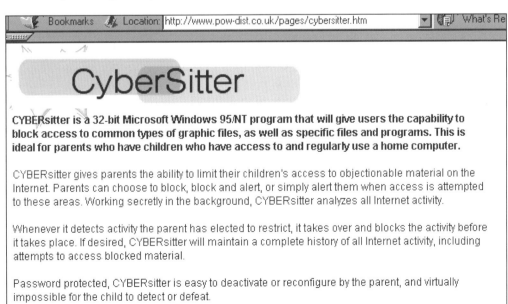

Location: http://www.pow-dist.co.uk/pages/cybersitter.htm

CyberSitter

CYBERsitter is a 32-bit Microsoft Windows 95/NT program that will give users the capability to block access to common types of graphic files, as well as specific files and programs. This is ideal for parents who have children who have access to and regularly use a home computer.

CYBERsitter gives parents the ability to limit their children's access to objectionable material on the Internet. Parents can choose to block, block and alert, or simply alert them when access is attempted to these areas. Working secretly in the background, CYBERsitter analyzes all Internet activity.

Whenever it detects activity the parent has elected to restrict, it takes over and blocks the activity before it takes place. If desired, CYBERsitter will maintain a complete history of all Internet activity, including attempts to access blocked material.

Password protected, CYBERsitter is easy to deactivate or reconfigure by the parent, and virtually impossible for the child to detect or defeat.

Protecting children ....

Rating systems

A rating system is based on an internationally agreed set of tools that can be used to control who sees what kind of content. Web sites rate themselves and include the rating information hidden on their web pages. People's browsers (Internet Explorer, Netscape etc) then access this information and determine whether the site is acceptable to the user or not. Sites rated as carrying unacceptable content are not shown. For the rating system to work, you must be using a browser capable of being configured for ratings, and you must set these rating to the levels of tolerance you want it to exert.

▶ *Action* – In Microsoft's Internet Explorer, you can find the rating system in 'Tools', 'Internet Options', 'Content' and 'Content Advisor'. Once you enable content advisor, a password is needed to bypass it.

Platform for Internet Content Selection (PICS) is now widely accepted as the main way to implement these rating. The most used set of standards for screening material was developed by the Recreational Software Advisory Council on the Internet (RSACi). This rates material according to the degree of sex, violence, nudity, and bad language depicted. The levels and categories of the PICS/RSACi rating are shown in the table below.

The vast majority of sites on the web do not, and may never, use any ratings so, unless you allow your browser software to view unrated sites, your child will be blocked from many of the best sites on the web.

The problem of censoring internet content with a system like PICS is that there will always be conflicts of interest. Will pro-life activists want to ban abortion sites? Will pro-abortion supporters want to ban anti-abortion sites? What about animal cruelty and the question of fox hunting? The problem is not whether such sites should be filtered out, it is

Level	Violence	Nudity	Sex	Language
0	Harmless conflict, some damage to objects.	No nudity or revealing attire.	Romance, no sex.	Inoffensive slang; no profanity.
1	Creatures injured or killed; damage to objects; fighting.	Revealing attire.	Passionate kissing.	Mild expletives.
2	Humans injured, or small amounts of blood.	Partial nudity.	Clothed sexual touching.	Expletives; non-sexual anatomical references.
3	Humans injured or killed.	Non-sexual frontal nudity.	Non-explicit sexual activity.	Strong, vulgar language; obscene gestures; racial epithets.
4	Wanton and gratuitous violence; torture; rape.	Provocative frontal nudity.	Explicit sexual activity; sex crimes.	Crude or explicit sexual references; extreme hate speech.

who will do the filtering? With PICS, the decision is largely taken out of your hands. Whatever the standards, you will lose out on great resources.

The rating system is also politically sensitive, because internet cafés and schools are increasingly forcing users to have PICS enabled if they wish to use their machines and browsers. This is little more than covert censorship of publicly available information. For more information, go to the Internet Freedom site at http://www.netfreedom.org/uk. Internet Freedom is 'opposed to all attempts to censor and regulate the internet from newsgroup bans to the use of PICS'.

Besides, both Internet Explorer and Netscape are easy to bypass by any intelligent teenager, who will probably regard it as a challenge. See page 131.

Parental control

A third approach relies on parental guidance and education. As with a television, if a computer is in the child's bedroom, there is no way of ensuring that your child is not accessing something dubious or harmful. Always assume that your child knows more about the internet than you do. Unfortunately, the child may not have the common sense to avoid being harmed or conned by someone or by a web site on the internet.

Sharing the experience of the internet with your children will help you obtain the full benefits and alert you to any potential problems that may await your child. If your children tell you about an upsetting incident, don't blame them. It is unlikely to be their fault. Help them to understand what has happened. How you respond to the problem will determine whether they confide in you the next time.

Fig. 70. RightTrack gives in-depth advice and information about issues of child safety on the internet. This is a very good site – make it your first port of call if you are responsible for children who use the internet.

Company Info
Home
Profile
Instructors
Clients
Testimonials
News
Contact Us

Training
Description
Courses
Class Schedule
Registration
Seminars

Other Services
Tech Support
Networks
App Development
Web Design
Classroom Rentals
Membership

RIGHT-TRACK
L E A R N I N G   C E N T E R

Child Safety Links

Keeping children safe from harm is crucial to giving them the advantages of Internet access. Here are some links that explore the topic of child safety, including a few of the many "child-friendly" sites.

Information for Parents:

Child Safety on the Information Highway is probably the best and best-known writing on the subject. Written by Lawrence J. Magid, a syndicated columnist for the Los Angeles Times, this article separates the myths from the realities, explains what the risks are, includes guidelines for parents, and rules for children to abide by while on the Net.

Family PC's Kid Safety Clearinghouse, links regarding violence on the Net, Internet access at school and "kid-friendly" Net utilities.

Protecting children ....

Never allow a computer with internet access to remain in a child's bedroom. Besides making the child unsociable, it can be an open invitation for strangers. Keep the computer in a shared room. Keep an eye on what is happening or, even better, join in. If all else fails, you can lock it away when you leave the child alone in the house for any length or time.

Educate your children so that they know not to give out personal information such as name, address, phone number, email address, and name of school to anyone or any site on the internet without talking to you first.

You may have taught your child to avoid strangers in the street, but what is a stranger on the internet? Make sure that your child understands that a web site can collect information by using cartoon characters to act as representatives. Would your child trust his favourite cartoon character? How can a red fluffy bunny or a funny-faced clown possibly be harmful?

If a total stranger stopped your child in the street and asked all kinds of personal questions about your family, you would be shocked. You might even report the incident to the police. But once your child goes on the internet the chance is that far more personal information will be asked for regularly and by many different 'strangers'.

Tips for the kids

Some things you should NEVER do

1. Accept gifts or money from anybody.
2. Respond to messages or bulletin board items that are suggestive, obscene, belligerent, threatening, or make you feel uncomfortable.
3. Agree to a meeting.
4. Open or accept emails, files, links, URLs, or other things from people you don't really know or trust.
5. Give out your password to anyone except your parents or guardian, not even to your best friend.

Some things you MUST tell your parents or guardian about:
1. If someone tries to arrange a face to face meeting.
2. If you come across any information that makes you feel uncomfortable. Don't try to respond, just tell your parents.
3. Someone asks you to about personal information such as your name, address, school, or telephone number.
4. If someone asks you to send a picture of yourself.

Remember that people online may not be who they seem. Since you can't see or even hear the person it would be easy for that person to misrepresent him or herself. Someone you think is a twelve-year-old child may be an adult using someone else's picture, name, and age.

Government control

Can any national government make the internet safe for children within their borders? It is doubtful unless some kind of global control is exerted over internet content. Yet global control would seem both impossible and undesirable. Censoring the internet will simply not work without destroying its very nature and value. When governments legislate, they tend to do so with sledgehammer ferocity, often in response to hysterical headlines.

The most effective method of law enforcement in this area seems to be for dedicated police officers to pretend to be young people and try to attract the paedophiles. According to the police, once a paedophile has been identified, they are easy to catch because they tend to be obsessive and run headlong into the traps.

Once a target has been identified, the police have access to many different techniques of evidence collection. These include the records of ISPs, and seizing the accused person's computer to extract evidence from the hard disk. There are even sophisticated surveillance techniques that enable police experts to remotely view what is on a person's computer monitor and even record the keystrokes they type.

Nor does the fact that a perpetrator lives or operates in a foreign country mean they can always escape justice. A ruling about this was made in November 1999 by Judge Christopher Hardy at Southwark Crown Court. He said that a web pornographer could be prosecuted for publishing material declared illegal under the UK's Obscene Publications Act, despite the fact that his server was in the US. The fact that an obscene picture was downloaded within the UK meant that it was published within the UK even though the server was in the USA.

TRUSTe system

You will at some time come across sites that have a seal of approval (in the form of a seal balancing a ball) issued by TRUSTe. A web site displaying the TRUSTe Children's Seal must agree to certain requirements before displaying the seal. If directed at children aged thirteen or under, the site will:

1. Collect personal information from the child only with parental consent.

2. Give parents the opportunity to prevent use of the information.

3. In the absence of consent, personal information shall not be used to re-contact the child for other purposes.

4. Only distribute personal information about a child to third parties after parental consent.

5. Only give the child the ability to give out personally identifiable contact information after parental consent.

6. Make best efforts to prohibit a child from posting any contact information.

7. Not use a special games, prizes or other activities to entice a child to give away more information than is needed to participate in that activity.

8. Place a notice on any page that requests personally identifiable information requesting that the child talk to a parent or guardian before answering the questions.

Many sites make only a token gesture towards obtaining parental consent and children can easily get around the limitations. TRUSTe stresses that before a site earns the seal, it must ensure that it obtains *verifiable* parental consent before information is collected, as well as telling parents how the information will be used. TRUSTe also regularly reviews the sites in their program to make sure the site is not violating its privacy statement.

Case studies

The perils of auctions
In April 1999 *The Times* reported that a 13-year-old computer buff had run up a bill of £1.8 million on the internet. The boy had started out by trying to sell his friend as a slave on an online auctioneers called eBay. Although nobody bought his friend, he was bitten by the auction bug and started to bid for goods himself. Three weeks later, the goods that he had bought included a 1955 sports car for $23,000, a Ford Convertible for $24,500, and a bed from Canada worth $900,000. The boy admitted to journalists that he was in 'big trouble' with his mother.

It was first believed that he used his parents' password to gain access to eBay. Later it was reported that he had his own account with eBay. The moral: always assume that your children's intelligence will exceed their sense of responsibility. The only precaution that the parents could have used in this case would have been to exercise some guidance, and take better security with their passwords.

US censorship
Teachers and students at New York City schools are disturbed that a broad filtering program on their computer system is making legitimate class work suffer. A filter (called I-Gear from Urlabs) is being used to block access to undesirable sites. Unfortunately, it also blocks many of the major newsgroups, policy groups, and scientific and medical organisations. Students at a high school in Queens, for example, were researching an assignment on health issues. They received 'Access Denied' messages when trying to visit sites on breast cancer, eating disorders, childbirth, AIDS, and abortion. Many of the schools have had problems with the filter and have filed complaints with the New York Civil Liberties Union.

Porn publisher charged
At Southwark Crown Court, London, in 1999 Judge Christopher Hardy ruled that 28-year-old Graham Waddon could be prosecuted for publishing material declared illegal under the UK's Obscene Publications Act, one of the most illiberal in the western world, even though Waddon had placed that material on servers in the USA.

How children bypass the ratings filters (or you if you forget the password):

1. Netscape is simple: all you need to do is uninstall and reinstall Netscape Navigator.

2. Internet Explorer is a little more difficult. In Windows, go to Start, then Run, and get ready to edit the Windows Registry by typing in REGEDIT.EXE. Delete[1] the key in:

   HKEY_LOCAL MACHINE\SOFTWARE\MICROSOFT\WINDOWS\ CURRENT VERSION\POLICIES\RATINGS

   Then use Windows Explorer to delete the file C:\WINDOWS\ SYSTEM\RATINGS.POL. Now reboot the computer.

Finding out more
You can find out more about this topic by using any search engine.

For details of other filtering software, see Peacefire at:
http://www.peacefire.org

Also, see *Protecting Children on the Internet* by Graham Jones (Internet Handbooks).

Visit the free Internet HelpZone at
www.internet-handbooks.co.uk
Helping you master the internet

---

1. If you decide to try this, make sure you back up your registry first.

8 Privacy organisations and resources

In this chapter we will explore:

▶ *usenet: cryptography, privacy and security*
▶ *child protection organisations on the web*
▶ *civil rights and pro privacy groups on the web*
▶ *government organisations on the web*
▶ *password software*
▶ *cookie cutters*
▶ *anti-virus software*
▶ *anti-spam software*
▶ *encryption software*
▶ *patches and fixes*
▶ *other useful programs*

Usenet: cryptography

Here are the leading newsgroups dedicated to researching and testing PGP encryption (see page 104 for more about PGP):

alt.security.pgp
comp.security.pgp.announce
comp.security.pgp.discuss
comp.security.pgp.resources
comp.security.pgp.tech
comp.security.pgp.test

sci.crypt
This newsgroup considers scientific and social issues of cryptography. Example topics include the legitimate use of PGP, public-key patents, DES, cryptographic security, and cipher breaking.

Usenet: privacy

alt.privacy
This group discusses general privacy issues involving government eavesdropping, taxpaying, licensing, social security numbers, and similar topics.

alt.privacy.anon-server
This one mainly contains conversations on anonymous servers. If you want to view web sites or send email privately, this is the group to subscribe to and, if you are having any problems, you will find plenty of helpful people hanging around.

comp.society.privacy
The group considers privacy issues associated with computer technologies. Example topics include: caller identification, social security numbers, credit applications, and mailing lists. This is a moderated group (junk mail and irrelevant posts are removed/ filtered) so you can be assured that the posts remain relevant to computer privacy issues.

Usenet: security

alt.computer.security
The group contains discussions of computer security in general. Topics include securing PCs against theft, protecting data, encrypting computer files, and so on.

comp.security.misc
Subscribers of this group discuss computer-related security issues similar to the above but with many more people and more technical discussions.

Child protection organisations on the web

CyberAngels
http://www.cyberangels.org
CyberAngels is actively engaged in protecting and educating children in internet safety. It has many useful resources such as a cyberstalking helpline and a Cybermoms approved safe site list for concerned parents. 'This in an important first...the first time a cross-industry group has launched a joint project, where we put children, not our egos first.' The site also contains advice and information on the more common problems encountered by children such as bullying at school.

Fig. 71. Cyberangels has an informative site. It is a pressure group and resource for parents, children and teachers concerned about the safety aspects of the internet.

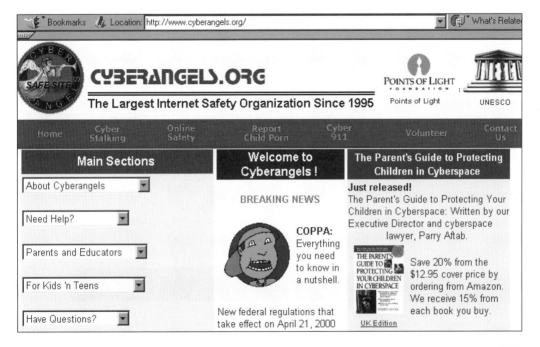

Privacy organisations and resources ....

Fig. 72. Peacefire 'liberates' youngsters by showing them step-by-step how to disable or bypass the filtering software that some parents and schools install on the computers they use.

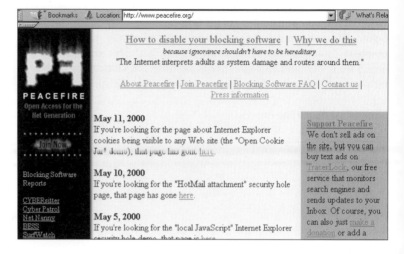

Peacefire

http://www.peacefire.org

Peacefire offers support and news concerning freedom of speech on the internet to young people under 18. Created in August 1996, it now has more than 3,000 members on its mailing list. Peacefire is run by staff who are almost all teenagers, although some of the older ones are starting to turn 20. The first content to be published informed members of some of the web sites that were blocked by popular filtering programs such as Cyber Patrol and Cybersitter. Since that time, Peacefire has helped lawyers to challenge library internet censorship policies in America.

Civil rights and pro-privacy groups on the web

Amnesty International

http://www.amnesty.org.uk

Amnesty aims to promote general awareness of human rights and oppose specific abuses of human rights. The values it upholds are

Fig. 73. Amnesty International was launched by a British lawyer in 1961. He was motivated by reading a news feature about some Portuguese students who had received seven-year prison sentences for raising their glasses in a toast to freedom.

contained in the Universal Declaration of Human Rights. It works through education activities and encouraging governments and other political bodies to support and respect human rights. Amnesty also encourages private and corporate organisations. They are probably most noted for their research and action against countries that imprison and torture people for political, cultural or religious reasons.

Cyber-Rights and Cyber-Liberties (UK)
http://www.cyber-rights.org
Cyber-Rights & Cyber-Liberties provides updates on the UK government's latest encryption policies. The site offers reports, press releases and information about campaigns, and news items related to UK and overseas privacy policy. Developments within the US and the European Union are also closely monitored.

Cyber-Rights
http://www.cyber-rights.org/eu-watch
Cyber-Rights & Cyber-Liberties monitors European Union policy and legal initiatives in relation to the internet. These initiatives mainly deal with attempts to regulate illegal and harmful content over the internet, the development of ecommerce, encryption and digital signatures policy, internet service providers' liability, and intellectual property rights.

Directory of Human Rights Resources on the Internet
http://shr.aaas.org/dhr.htm
The Directory provides descriptions and links to hundreds of independently maintained human rights organisations all over the world on the internet.

Electronic Frontier Foundation (EFF)
http://www.eff.com
The EFF - 'the leading civil libertarians of the digital age' - is a non-profit organisation that works to protect freedom of speech and promote responsibility on the internet. The following is from their mission statement:
'A new world is arising in the vast web of digital, electronic media

Fig. 74. The Electronic Frontier Foundation (EFF) is a sort of Amnesty International of cyberspace. Its slogan is: 'Protecting rights and promoting freedom in the electronic frontier.'

135

which connect us. Computer-based communication media like electronic mail and computer conferencing are becoming the basis of new forms of community. These communities without a single, fixed geographical location comprise the first settlements on an electronic frontier.

'While well-established legal principles and cultural norms give structure and coherence to uses of conventional media like newspapers, books, and telephones, the new digital media do not so easily fit into existing frameworks. Conflicts come about as the law struggles to define its application in a context where fundamental notions of speech, property, and place take profoundly new forms. People sense both the promise and the threat inherent in new computer and communications technologies, even as they struggle to master or simply cope with them in the workplace and the home.

'The Electronic Frontier Foundation has been established to help civilise the electronic frontier; to make it truly useful and beneficial not just to a technical elite, but to everyone; and to do this in a way which is in keeping with our society's highest traditions of the free and open flow of information and communication.'

Electronic Privacy Information Centre (EPIC)
http://www.epic.org
EPIC is a research centre in Washington. It was established in 1994 to focus public attention on civil liberties issues and to protect privacy, the First Amendment, and constitutional values. EPIC works in association with the London human rights group Privacy International.

Internet Freedom
http://www.netfreedom.org
Internet Freedom is opposed to all forms of censorship and content regulation on the net. The site mainly consists of news items about the many forms of censorship being attempted around the world.

Privacy International
http://www.privacyinternational.org
Their site says: 'Privacy International is a human rights group formed in 1990 as a watchdog on surveillance by governments and corporations.

Fig. 75. Privacy International is an activist organisation. It keeps a beady eye on the relentless global rise of government eavesdropping, and on personal privacy violations by all kinds of other organisations.

PI is based in London, UK and has an office in Washington DC. PI has conducted campaigns in Europe, Asia and North America to counter abuses of privacy by way of information technology such as telephone tapping, ID card systems, video surveillance, data matching, police information systems, and medical records.'

Fig. 76. The Privacy Page logo.

The Privacy Page
http://www.privacy.org
There is mainly American news on the site, but there is plenty of it, and it's good quality. Since the policies and events in the US often have repercussions for other countries, it is a good site to refer to if you want to see the bigger picture.

Privacy Rights Clearing House
http://www.privacyrights.org
The PRC site provides in-depth information on a variety of informational privacy issues, as well as giving tips on safeguarding your personal privacy. The PRC was established with funding from the Telecommunications Education Trust, a program of the California Public Utilities Commission.

Fig. 77. Statewatch works on similar lines to Privacy International, but concentrates on civil liberties issues inside the European Union. It puts more emphasis on privacy violations in areas other than the internet.

Statewatch
http://www.statewatch.org
Statewatch monitors the activities of governments and various threats to civil liberties in the European Union. It reports on policing, security and intelligence agencies, prisons, military activities, immigration and asylum issues, racism and fascism, openness and secrecy, FBI surveillance system, Northern Ireland, and civil liberties in general.

Privacy organisations and resources ....

Government organisations on the web

The Data Protection Registrar
http://www.dpr.gov.uk
The Data Protection Registrar maintains a list of UK companies that have announced that they use information about employees or customers. The site has a complete copy of the public register and is updated weekly. You can search the register here.

Fig. 78. The UK Data Protection Registrar is there to help the citizen. However, the new UK Freedom of Information Act (or should it be Freedom *from* Information Act?) makes politicians and bureaucrats exempt from revealing just about anything they do not wish to reveal.

EU Directive on Data Protection
http://www.hmso.gov.uk/acts/acts1998/19980029.htm
In 1984, the UK Data Protection Act was passed. This gives individuals the right to see information held about themselves on computers but not necessarily police or government computers. In 1998, the right to privacy was written into the European Convention on Human Rights in Article 8. The Directive establishes guidelines intended to ensure a high level of protection for the privacy of individuals and the free movement of personal data within the European Union. Under the Directive, you have a number of rights and can appeal to independent national authorities if you think those rights are being denied. These rights include:

1. Access to information about where the data originated or where such information is available.

2. The right to know which organisation is processing data about you and why.

3. Access to personal data relating to you.

4. The ability to change personal information about you that is inaccurate.

5. The right to stop the organisation using information about you in certain circumstances (for example, for direct marketing purposes, without providing any specific reason).

Sensitive information such as your ethnic or racial origin, political or religious beliefs, trade union membership or information about your health or sexual life can only be used with your consent. There are a number of exemptions for specific cases such as where there is an important public interest (e.g. for medical or scientific research) and where alternative safeguards have to be established. You can read the wording of the Act at this site.

Password software

Password Creator
http://www.infokeep.net/pc/
Password Creator is 'the password generation utility used by the US Pentagon joint staff.' Sounds pretty good, and it's free.

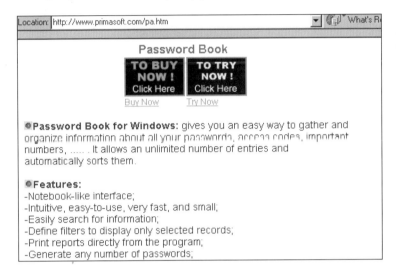

Fig. 79. Password Creator can take much of the work out of trying to make your passwords secure.

Password Generator
http://ourworld.compuserve.com/homepages/hirtle
'Simply the most secure method for creating passwords. Voted by Windows Magazine as "Superior Shareware" (Aug 1995).' The Password Generator will randomly select from a group of numbers, lower case letters, upper case letters and special characters or any combination and select passwords. You can generate up to 1,000,000 different passwords, using as many as 25 characters each. The generator uses numbers, upper and lower case letters, and special keyboard characters. You can identify exactly which characters to let the program use for the random selection process and you can also apply rules that will prevent the same character being used repeatedly and prevent the use of sequential characters such as 'abc' or '123'.

Password Book
http://www.primasoft.com
Password Book is an information manager that lets you easily keep track of all your passwords, access codes, and important numbers. You can quickly locate and retrieve information, print it, sort by different fields, generate new passwords, and more. All records are sorted alphabetically by any field so you can find them easily. The program organises the data efficiently, so that the information is readily accessible in a variety of ways. A similar format to a physical notebook makes the program very easy to use, intuitive, and straightforward. Online help messages are only a mouse click away. It can be used by both beginners and advanced users. Your application can be protected with a password. Only

those who know the password will be able to access your data. Your data file stored on a hard disk is encrypted.

Cookie cutters

Anti-Cookie	Windows	http://users.derbytech.com/~gregeng/cookie10.zip
CookieCutter	Windows	http://ayecor.com/software/cc32/oopo32.zip
Cookie Monster	MacOS	http://www.geocities.com/Paris/1778/CookieMonster151.sit
Cookie? NOT!	Windows	http://www.geocities.com/SiliconValley/Vista/2665/bake.zip
Cookie Pal	Windows	http://www.kburra.com/cp1setup.exe
NoMoreCookies	MacOS	http://www.chelmsford.com/home/star/software/downloads/no_more_cookies.sit.bin
ScapeGoat	MacOS	ftp://ftp.stazsoftware.com/pub/downloads/scapegoat.sea.hqx

Anti-virus software

F-Prot
http://www.isvr.soton.ac.uk/ftp/pc/f-prot
You can download the latest F-Prot from here.

Download
http://download.cnet.com
At this site you can download other free anti-virus software, such as Disinfectant for Macintosh and trial versions of commercial anti-virus software.

Further sources
Some further information on viruses and scanners can be found at:

http://www.drsolomon.com
http://www.datafellows.com
http://www.datarescue.com
http://www.metro.ch/avpve

Anti-spam software

Spam Buster
http://www.contactplus.com/index2.htm
Spam Buster (Windows 95) has an editable list of over 15,000 spam sources. It can check up to 12 email accounts automatically at periods that you decide. Spam Buster costs $19.95 to register.

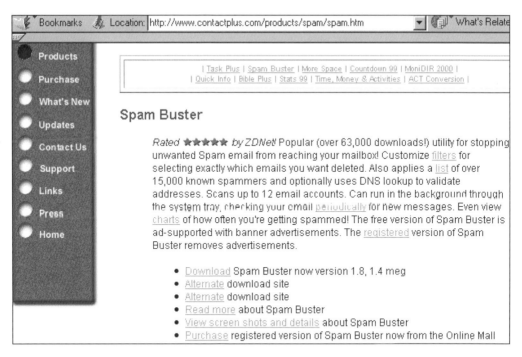

Fig. 80. Spam Buster is a beefed-up filter that works with most common email programs. It's a kind of virtual bouncer working on your behalf.

Spam Hater

http://www.compulink.co.uk/~net-services/spam

Spam Hater (Windows 95) is free software that helps you respond effectively to spammers. It analyses the spam, extracts a list of addresses of relevant postmasters, prepares a reply, gives you a choice of legal threats, insults, or your own message, and appends a copy of the spam if required. It also helps you to analyse Usenet spam.

SpamKiller

http://www.spamkiller.com

SpamKiller (Windows 95) filters your email against a large list of known spam sources, subjects, and headers. SpamKiller is shareware. You can try it free for 30 days then pay $29.95 to register it.

Fig. 81. Not content with a bouncer? Hire Spam Killer, a real tough guy when it comes to combatting spam.

141

Privacy organisations and resources ....

Mail Guard

http://www.fundi.com/index.html

Mail Guard (Windows 95 or Windows NT 4.0) blocks messages from unapproved people. Mail Guard, and costs $20 to register. Mail Guard separates people who send you email into two categories a black list and a white list. You enter any spammers into the black list and others are put into the white list. Mail Guard checks your mailbox and removes any emails from the black list and then opens your email program to handle the rest in the normal way.

Encryption software

The International PGP Home Page

http://www.pgpi.org

At this site, you can download the latest freeware PGP version for your system. It also shows you where to buy the latest commercial version.

Scramdisk

http://www.scramdisk.clara.net

Scramdisk allows you to create and use virtual encrypted drives. Basically, you create a large file on an existing hard disk, which is created and encrypted with a password. This file is then treated as an extra hard disk by your system. Scramdisk creates a new drive letter to represent the 'virtual' disk. This new disk can then only be accessed with the correct password. Scramdisk is free.

Fig. 82. If your computer is likely to be used, or acquired in the future, by other people, you should consider encrypting all your sensitive files. Scramdisk is a highly secure method of protecting your work.

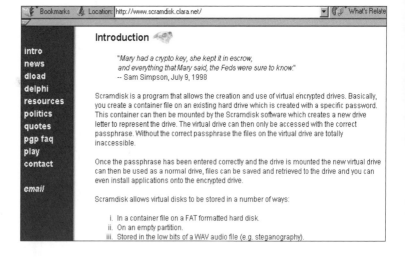

BestCrypt

http://www.jetico.sci.fi

BestCrypt secures the data on your hard drive with military-strength encryption without the complexities normally associated with strong data encryption. You can try it for 30 days, then pay about $90 for a licence. The program is very easy to use.

East-Tec Eraser
http://www.east-tec.com
East-Tec Eraser is an advanced security application designed to completely eliminate sensitive data from your computer. You can automatically clear the contents of folders that usually contain sensitive data (your web browser cache, Temporary Internet files, cookies, history, and recent document list). You can also erase entire folder structures and even entire drives. The number of passes specifies how many times to overwrite the data. One pass is sufficient to stop software recovery tools. Several passes might be needed to stop hardware recovery tools such as electron-tunnelling microscopes. These tools can recover faint magnetic residue from previous writes. You are invited to evaluate Eraser for up to 30 days, at which time you are asked to register the software or discontinue its use. The software is available in several versions ranging from $19.95 to $39.95.

PGPWord
http://ourworld.compuserve.com/homepages/TSSINFO
PGPWord is a Windows 95 program that integrates with Microsoft Word. It encodes your documents with military strength PGP encryption. Once you have entered your password, PGPWord automatically encrypts and decrypts documents as you open and close them. It costs $19.95 to register PGPWord.

Patches and fixes

Hewlett Packard ActiveX fixes
http://www.systemsoft.com/support/syswiz/index.htm
SystemSoft provides a patch to fix the security holes in some Hewlett Packard systems. Download it from here.

Microsoft security patches
http://www.microsoft.com/security/bulletins/

Fig. 83. The Microsoft Security Bulletin is an excellent source of information and fixes. The site is essential if you want to keep up-to-date about security holes in Microsoft products, and how to deal with them.

Privacy organisations and resources ....

Other useful programs

AtGuard

http://www.atguard.com/product.info

AtGuard helps you surf faster, keep your personal information private, and control access by others to your PC. AtGuard lets you surf faster by blocking out annoying advertisements, graphics and animated GIFs. It also lets you protect your privacy by blocking cookies and preventing web sites from tracking the 'referrer' (previous web pages that you visit). AtGuard also comes with a personal firewall that lets you control who can access your PC, and you can choose whether to run JavaScripts, ActiveX controls, and Java applets on your computer.

Opera

http://www.operasoftware.com

Opera is a great web browser that gives you more control over your browsing. 'If you use the web for work and not for entertainment, Opera is by far the best choice you can make.' Opera is very efficient at using the internet for research. You can do things like open multiple windows without running out of memory, redirect output from one window to another, toggle document and user settings, retrieve all documents in a hotlist folder, and zoom in and out of the pages. There is more to browsing than just Internet Explorer and Netscape.

Proxomitron

http://proxomitron.tripod.com

Proxomitron uses special filters to change web pages as you browse. You can speed up your browsing by rejecting slow loading adverts and other web junk. 'Take control of your web viewing, and don't be slave to some web-master's whims,' it says on the site. Some of the things you can do are:

1. Stop web pages and ads from auto-refreshing.
2. Remove Dynamic HTML.
3. Prevent getting stuck in someone's frames.
4. Remove frames or tables altogether.
5. Kill or change selected Java scripts and applets.
6. Add your own scripts to pages.
7. Remove or replace web page and/or table background images.

Finally ...

Powerful privacy tools and resources of almost every kind imaginable are out there on the internet somewhere. Use the search engines and the specialist newsgroups to track down what you want.

Further online references

General

Glossary of Internet Terms
http://www.matisse.net/files/glossary.html
For an extensive glossary of internet terms look at this site. See also the glossary in this book.

Internet Security
http://www.tiac.net/users/smiths/security/index.htm
This site has lots of scary, but safe, demonstrations of the many security holes in internet browsers and email programs.

Microsoft Security Advisor
http://www.microsoft.com/security/default.asp
A good site for security news and information, especially related to Microsoft's own programs. This is the main site for fixes to Internet Explorer and Outlook Express.

Netscape's Security Home Page
http://www.netscape.com/products/security/
This is Netscape's security page for those of you who use Netscape Navigator.

Scott Schnoll's Unofficial IE4 Security FAQ
http://www.nwnetworks.com/iesf.html
Here you will find a more unofficial viewpoint of Microsoft's security in relation to Internet Explorer 4.0.

Pentium III serial numbers: news stories

ABCNews
http://abcnews.go.com/sections/tech/DailyNews/pentiumdebut990218.html
Controversial Pentium III debuts: Intel officials focus on performance, critics on privacy. February 18, 1999.

CNET
http://www.news.com/News/Item/Textonly/0,25,32499,00.html
Pentium III preview gets muted greeting. February 17, 1999.

CNET
http://www.news.com/News/Item/0,4,32331,00.html
What does Pentium III bring to the party? February 11, 1999.

CNNFN
http://www.cnnfn.com/digitaljam/9902/18/intel/
Pentium III battle persists: Privacy groups say Intel misled public regarding chip's security feature. February 18, 1999.

Further online references......................................

InformationWeek
http://www.techweb.com/wire/story/TWB19990217S0007
Privacy groups threaten to boycott Intel. February 17, 1999.

Reuters
http://dailynews.yahoo.com/headlines/tc/story.html?s=v/nm/19990216/tc/
intel.1.html
Intel to launch Pentium III amid privacy protests. February 16, 1999.

Reuters NetTrends
http://dailynews.yahoo.com/headlines/wr/story.html?s=v/nm/19990217/wr/
nettrends.16.html
An arms race in computer privacy. February 17, 1999.

Wired News
http://www.wired.com/news/news/technology/story/18139.html
Pentium III draws more fire. February 25, 1999.

ZDNet
http://www.zdnet.com/zdnn/stories/news/0,4586,2217603,00.html
Is Intel not paranoid enough? Why the chip giant is losing the sales race to upstart
AMD. February 25, 1999.

Anonymity

Anonymizer
http://www.anonymizer.com
This is a very useful site that lets you surf without leaving a trail of personal
information across the web. This service offers unlimited free trial access.
Anonymizer also offers a free anonymous email service.

Ghost Mail
http://www.geocities.com/SunsetStrip/Villa/7632/ghostmail.htm
This is a freeware Windows utility that allows you to send anonymous messages,
with or without a remailer, to any email address or to Usenet newsgroups.

HushMail
http://www.hushmail.com
Are you worried about the privacy of your email? You should be, given the security
woes that plague email these days. HushMail is a free web-based email service that
uses 1024-bit encryption. Your recipient must also be a HushMail user. The service
only supports Windows at time of writing, but a Mac version was being planned for
the near future.

Remailer lists
http://www.cs.berkely.edu/~ralph/remailer-list.html
You will find a comprehensive list of remailers at this site.

ZipLip
https://www.ziplip.com
If you need to send a confidential email try this free service. ZipLip uses advanced encryption techniques to protect your confidentiality. When you send a message from ZipLip, it is protected by a password stored in an encrypted format. Only when your recipient supplies the correct password is your message decrypted and delivered to the recipient.

Cookies

Andy's HTTP Cookie Info
http://www.illuminatus.com/cookie.fcgi

Malcolm's Guide to Persistent Cookies
http://www.emf.net/ ~ mal/cookiesinfo.html

Passwords

The Passphrase FAQ
http://www.stack.urc.tue.nl/ ~ galactus/remailers/passphrase-faq.html

Spam

Blacklist of Internet Advertisers
http://math-www.uni-paderborn.de/ ~ axel/BL

Coalition Against Unsolicited Commercial Email
http://www.cauce.org

Dealing with Junk Email
http://www.metareality.com/ ~ nathan/visit.cgi/html.JunkMail

Everything You'd Rather Not Have To Know About Net-Abuse
http://www.tezcat.com/ ~ haz1/netabuse/netabuse.html

Filtering Mail FAQ
http://www.jazzie.com/ii/faqs/archive/mail/filtering-faq

JunkBusters
http://www.junkbusters.com

Net Abuse FAQ
http://www.cybernothing.org/faqs/net-abuse-faq.html

John Rivard's Stop Junk E-Mail Page
http://www.mcs.net/ ~ jcr/junkemail.html

Tips Specific to AOL
http://www.markwelch.com/aol.junk.htm

Glossary

access provider – The company that provides you with access to the internet. This may be an independent provider or a large international organisation such as AOL or CompuServe. See also **internet service provider**.

ActiveX – A programming language that allows effects such as animations, games and other interactive features to be included a web page.

Adobe Acrobat – A type of software required for reading PDF files ('portable document format'). You may need to have Adobe Acrobat Reader when downloading large text files from the internet, such as lengthy reports or chapters from books. If your computer lacks it, the web page will prompt you, and usually offer you an immediate download of the free version.

address book – A directory in a web browser where you can store people's email addresses. This saves having to type them out each time you want to email someone. You just click on an address whenever you want it.

AltaVista – One of the half dozen most popular internet search engines. Just type in a few key words to find what you want: http://www.altavista.com

AOL – America On Line, the world's biggest internet service provider, with more than 20 million subscribers, and now merged with Time Warner. Because it has masses of content of its own – quite aside from the wider internet – it is sometimes referred to as an 'online' service provider rather than internet service provider. It has given away vast numbers of free CDs with the popular computer magazines to build its customer base.

applet – An application programmed in Java that is designed to run only on a web browser. Applets cannot read or write data onto your computer, only from the domain in which they are served. When a web page using an applet is accessed, the browser will download it and run it on your computer. See also **Java**.

application – Any program, such as a word processor or spreadsheet program, designed for use on your computer.

ARPANET – Advanced Research Projects Agency Network, an early form of the internet.

ASCII – American Standard Code for Information Interchange. It is a simple text file format that can be accessed by most word processors and text editors. It is a universal file type for passing textual information across the internet.

Ask Jeeves – A popular internet search engine. Rather than just typing in a few key words for your search, you can type in a whole question or instruction, such as 'Find me everything about online investment.' It draws on a database of millions of questions and answers, and works best with fairly general questions.

ASP – Active Server Pages, a filename extension for a type of web page.

attachment – A file sent with an email message. The attached file can be anything from a word-processed document to a database, spreadsheet, graphic, or even a sound or video file. For example you could email someone birthday greetings, and attach a sound track or video clip.

Authenticode – Authenticode is a system where ActiveX controls can be authenticated in some way, usually by a certificate.

avatar – A cartoon or image used to represent someone on screen while taking part in internet chat.

backup – A second copy of a file or a set of files. Backing up data is essential if there is any risk of data loss.

bandwidth – The width of the electronic highway that gives you access to the internet. The higher the bandwidth, the wider this highway, and the faster the traffic can flow.

banner ad – This is a band of text and graphics, usually situated at the top of a web page. It acts like a title, telling the user what the content of the page is about. It invites the visitor to click on it to visit that site. Banner advertising has become big business.

baud rate – The data transmission speed in a modem, measured in bps (bits per second).

BBS – Bulletin board service. A facility to read and to post public messages on a particular web site.

binary numbers – The numbering system used by computers. It only uses 1s and 0s to represent numbers. Decimal numbers are based on the number 10. You can count from nought to nine. When you count higher than nine, the nine is replaced with a 10. Binary numbers are based on the number 2: each place can only have the value of 1 or 0. You can count from nought to one. When you count

higher than one, the one is replaced by 10 (not ten but one zero). Binary 10 would be equal to Decimal 2. For example:
Decimal 012345678910
Binary 01101110010111011100010011010

Blue Ribbon Campaign – A widely supported campaign supporting free speech and opposing moves to censor the internet by all kinds of elected and unelected bodies.

bookmark – A file of URLs of your favourite internet sites. Bookmarks are very easily created by bookmarking (mouse-clicking) any internet page you like the look of. If you are an avid user, you could soon end up with hundreds of them! In the Internet Explorer browser and AOL they are called 'favourites'.

boolean search A search in which you type in words such as AND and OR to refine your search. Such words are called 'Boolean operators'. The concept is named after George Boole, a nineteenth-century English mathematician.

bot – Short for robot. It is used to refer to a program that will perform a task on the internet, such as carrying out a search.

browser – Your browser is your window to the internet, and will normally supplied by your internet service provider when you first sign up. It is the program that you use to access the world wide web, and manage your personal communications and privacy when online. By far the two most popular browsers are Netscape Communicator and its dominant rival Microsoft Internet Explorer. You can easily swap. Both can be downloaded free from their web sites and are found on the CD roms stuck to the computer magazines. It won't make much difference which one you use – they both do much the same thing. Opera, at http://www.opera.com is a great alternative that improves security, is faster and more efficient.

bug – A weakness in a program or a computer system.

bulletin board – A type of computer-based news service that provides an email service and a file archive.

cache – A file storage area on a computer. Your web browser will normally cache (copy to your hard drive) each web page you visit. When you revisit that page on the web, you may in fact be looking at the page originally cached on your computer. To be sure you are viewing the current page, press **reload** – or **refresh** – on your browser toolbar. You can empty your cache from time to time, and the computer will do so automatically whenever the cache is full. In Internet Explorer, pages are saved in the Windows folder, Temporary Internet Files. In Netscape they are saved in a folder called 'cache'.

certificate – A computer file that securely identifies a person or organisation on the internet.

CGI (common gateway interface) – This defines how the web server should pass information to the program, such as what it's being asked to do, what objects it should work with, any inputs, and so on. It is the same for all web servers.

channel (chat) – Place where you can chat with other internet chatters. The name of a chat channel is prefixed with a hash mark, #.

click through – This is when someone clicks on a banner ad or other link, for example, and is moved from that page to the advertiser's web site.

client – This is the term given to the program that you use to access the internet. For example your web browser is a web client, and your email program is an email client.

community – The internet is often described as a net community. This refers to the fact that many people like the feeling of belonging to a group of like-minded individuals. Many big web sites have been developed along these lines, such as GeoCities which is divided into special-interest 'neighbourhoods', or America OnLine which is strong on member services.

compression – Computer files can be electronically compressed, so that they can be uploaded or downloaded more quickly across the internet, saving time and money. If an image file is compressed too much, there may be a loss of quality. To read them, you uncompress or 'unzip' them.

content – Articles, columns, sales messages, images, and the text of your web site.

content services – Web sites dedicated to a particular subject.

cookie – A cookie is a small code that the server asks your browser to keep until it asks for it. If it sends it with the first page and asks for it back before each other page, they can follow you around the site, even if you switch your computer off in between.

cracker – Someone who breaks into computer systems with the intention of causing some kind of damage or abusing the system in some way.

crash – What happens when a computer program malfunctions. The operating system of your PC may perform incorrectly or come to a complete stop ('freeze'), forcing you to shut down and restart.

cross-posting – Posting an identical message in several different newgroups at the same time.

cybercash – This is a trademark, but is also often used as a broad term to describe the use of small payments made over the internet using a new form of electronic account that is loaded up with cash. You can send this money to the companies offering such cash facilities by cheque, or by credit card. Some internet companies offering travel-related items can accept electronic cash of this kind.

cyberspace – Popular term for the intangible 'place' where you go to surf – the ethereal and borderless world of computers and telecommunications on the internet.

cypherpunk – From the cypherpunk mailing list charter: 'Cypherpunks assume privacy is a good thing and wish there were more of it. Cypherpunks acknowledge that those who want privacy must create it for themselves and not expect governments, corporations, or other large, faceless organisations to grant them privacy out of beneficence. Cypherpunks know that people have been creating their own privacy for centuries with whispers, envelopes, closed doors, and couriers. Cypherpunks do not seek to prevent other people from speaking about their experiences or their opinions.'

cypherpunk remailer – Cypherpunk remailers strip headers from the messages and add new ones.

data – Information. Data can exist in many forms such as numbers in a spreadsheet, text in a document, or as binary numbers stored in a computer's memory.

dial up account – This allows you to connect your computer to your internet provider's computer remotely.

digital – Based on the two binary digits, 1 and 0. The operation of all computers is based on this amazingly simple concept. All forms of information are capable of being digitalised – numbers, words, and even sounds and images – and then transmitted over the internet.

directory – On a PC, a folder containing your files.

DNS – Domain name server.

domain name – A name that identifies an IP address. It identifies to the computers on the rest of the internet where to access particular information. Each domain has a name. For someone@somewhere.co.uk, 'somewhere' is the domain name. The domain name for Internet Handbooks for instance is: www.internet-handbooks.co.uk

DotUK – One of the largest UK 'talkers'.

download – 'Downloading' means copying a file from one computer on the internet to your own computer. You do this by clicking on a button that links you to the appropriate file. Downloading is an automatic process, except you have to click 'yes' to accept the download and give it a file name. You can download any type of file – text, graphics, sound, spreadsheet, computer programs, and so on.

ebusiness – The broad concept of doing business to business, and business to consumer sales, over the internet.

ecash – Short for electronic cash. See cybercash.

ecommerce – The various means and techniques of transacting business online.

email – Electronic mail, any message or file you send from your computer to another computer using your 'email client' program (such as Netscape Messenger or Microsoft Outlook).

email address – The unique address given to you by your ISP. It can be used by others using the internet to send email messages to you. An example of a standard email address is: mybusiness@aol.com

email bomb – An attack by email where you are sent hundreds or thousands of email messages in a very short period. This attack often prevents you receiving genuine email messages.

emoticons – Popular symbols used to express emotions in email, for example the well known smiley :-) which means 'I'm smiling!' Emoticons are not normally appropriate for business communications.

encryption – The scrambling of information to make it unreadable without a key or password. Email and any other data can now be encrypted using PGP and other freely available programs. Modern encryption has become so amazingly powerful as to be to all intents and purposes uncrackable. Law enforcers worldwide are pressing their governments for access to people's and organisation's passwords and security keys. Would you be willing to hand over yours?

Excite – A popular internet directory and search engine used to find pages relating to specific keywords which you enter. See also Yahoo!.

ezines – The term for magazines and newsletters published on the internet.

FAQ – Frequently asked questions. You will see 'FAQ' everywhere you go on the internet. If you are ever doubtful about anything check the FAQ page, if the site has one, and you should find the answers to your queries.

favorites – The rather coy term for **bookmarks**, used by Internet Explorer, and by America Online. **Maintaining** a list of 'favourites' is designed to make returning to a site easier.

file – A file is any body of data such as a word processed document, a spreadsheet, a database file, a graphics or video file, sound file, or computer program.

filtering software – Software loaded onto a computer to prevent access by someone to unwelcome content on the internet, notably porn. The well-known 'parental controls' include CyberSitter, CyberPatrol, SurfWatch and NetNanny. They can be blunt instruments. For example, if they are programmed to reject all web pages containing the word 'virgin', you would not be able to access any web page hosted at Richard Branson's Virgin Net! Of course, there are also web sites that tell you step-by-step how to disable or bypass these filtering tools.

finger – A tool for locating people on the internet. The most common use is to see if a person has an account at a particular internet site. Also, a chat command which returns information about the other chat user, including idle time (time since they last did anything).

firewall – A firewall is special security software designed to stop the flow of certain files into and out of a computer network, e.g. viruses or attacks by hackers. A firewall would be an important feature of any fully commercial web site.

flame – A more or less hostile or aggressive message posted in a newsgroup or to an individual newsgroup user. If they get out of hand there can be flame wars.

folder – The name for a directory on a computer. It is a place in which files are stored.

form – A web page that allows or requires you to enter information into fields on the page and send the information to a web site, program or individual on the web. Forms are often used for registration or sending questions and comments to web sites.

forums – Places for discussion on the internet. They include Usenet newsgroups, mailing lists, and bulletin board services.

frames – A web design feature in which web pages are divided into several areas or panels, each containing separate information. A typical set of frames in a page includes an index frame (with navigation links), a banner frame (for a heading), and a body frame (for text matter).

freebies – The 'giveaway' products, services or other enticements offered on a web site to attract registrations.

freespace – An allocation of free web space by an internet service provider or other organisation, to its users or subscribers.

freeware – Software programs made available without charge. Where a small charge is requested, the term is **shareware**.

front page – The first page of your web site that the visitor will see. FrontPage is also the name of a popular web authoring package from Microsoft.

FTP – File transfer protocol the method the internet uses to speed files back and forth between computers. Your browser will automatically select this method, for instance, when you want to download your bank statements to reconcile your accounts. In practice you don't need to worry about FTP unless you are thinking about creating and publishing your own web pages: then you would need some of the freely available FTP software. Despite the name, it's easy to use.

GIF – A graphic information file. It is a compressed file format used on web pages and elsewhere to display files that contain graphic images. See also JPEG.

graphical client – A graphical client typically uses many windows, one for each conversation you are involved in. Each window has a command line and status bar.

GUI – Short for graphic user interface. It describes the user-friendly screens found in Windows and other WIMP environments (Windows, icons, mice, pointers).

hacker – A person interested in computer programming, operating systems, the internet and computer security. The term can be used to describe a person who breaks into computer systems with the intention of pointing out the weaknesses in a system. In common usage, the term is often wrongly used to describe crackers.

header – The header is that part of a message which contains information about the sender and the route that the message took through the internet.

history list – A record of visited web pages. Your browser probably includes a history list. It is handy way of revisiting sites whose addresses you have forgotten to bookmark – just click on the item you want in the history list. You

Glossary ....

can normally delete all or part of the history list in your browser. However, your ISP may well be keeping a similar list (see **internet service providers** – , above).

hit counter – A piece of software used by a web site to publicly display the number of hits it has received.

hits – The number of times a web page has been viewed.

home page – This refers to the index page of an individual or an organisation on the internet. It usually contains links to related pages of information, and to other relevant sites

host – A host is the computer where a particular file or domain is located, and from where people can retrieve it.

HotBot – A popular internet search engine used to find pages relating to any keywords you decide to enter.

html – Hypertext markup language, the universal computer language used to create pages on the world wide web. It is much like word processing, but uses special 'tags' for formatting the text and creating hyperlinks to other web pages.

http – Hypertext transfer protocol, the protocol used by the world wide web. It is the language spoken between your browser and the web servers. It is the standard way that HTML documents are transferred from host computer to your local browser when you're surfing the internet. You'll see this acronym at the start of every web address, e.g. http://www.abcxyz.com. With modern browsers, it is no longer necessary to enter 'http://' at the start of the address.

hyperlink – See **link**..

hypertext – This is a link on an HTML page that, when clicked with a mouse, results in a further HTML page or graphic being loaded into view on your browser.

Infoseek – One of the ten most popular internet search engines.

internet – The broad term for the fast-expanding network of global computers that can access each other in seconds by phone and satellite links. If you are using a modem on your computer, you too may be part of the internet. The general term 'internet' encompasses email, web pages, internet chat, newsgroups, and video conferencing. It is rather like the way we speak of 'the printed word' when we mean books, magazines, newspapers, newsletters, catalogues, leaflets, tickets and posters. The 'internet' does not exist in one place any more than 'the printed word' does.

internet account – The account set up by your internet service provider which gives you access to the world wide web, electronic mail facilities, newsgroups and other services.

Internet Explorer – The world's most popular browser software, a product of Microsoft and leading the field against Netscape (now owned by America OnLine).

internet service providers – ISPs are commercial, educational or official organisations which offer people ('users') access to the internet. The well-known commercial ones in the UK include AOL, CompuServe, BT Internet, Freeserve, Demon and Virgin Net. Commercial ISPs may levy a fixed monthly charge, though the world wide trend is now towards free services. Services typically include access to the world wide web, email and newsgroups, as well as others such as news, chat, and entertainment. Your internet service provider may know everything you do on the internet: emails sent and received, web sites visited, information downloaded, key words typed into search engines, newsgroups visited and messages read and posted. This is why many of them are willing to offer their services free. What do they do with all this data? How long do they store it? Do they make it discreetly available to enforcement agencies? Do they allow the police private access? There are some major issues of personal privacy and data protection in all this, at both a national and European level, and state surveillance is expanding fast. At the very least, check out your service provider's privacy statement – but it may mean very little.

Internic – The body responsible for allocating and maintaining internet domain names: http://www.internic.net

intranet – A private computer network that uses internet technology to allow communication between individuals, for example within a large commercial organisation. It often operates on a LAN (local area network).

IP address – An 'internet protocol' address. All computers linked to the internet have one. The address is somewhat like a telephone number, and consists of four sets of numbers separated by dots.

IRC – Internet relay chat. Chat is an enormously popular part of the internet, and there are all kinds of chat rooms and chat software. The chat involves typing messages which are sent and read in real time. It was developed in 1988 by a Finn called Jarkko Oikarinen.

ISDN – Integrated Services Digital Network. This is a high-speed telephone network that can send computer data from the internet to your PC faster than a normal telephone line.

Java – A programming language developed by Sun Microsystems to use the special properties of the internet to create graphics and multimedia applications on web sites.

JavaScript – A simple programming language that can be put onto a web page to create interactive effects such as buttons that change appearance when you position the mouse over them.

jpeg – The acronym is short for Joint Photographic Experts Group. A JPEG is a specialised file format used to display graphic files on the internet. JPEG files are smaller than similar GIF files and so have become ever more popular – even though there is sometimes a feeling that their quality is not as good as GIF format files. See also MPEG.

key shortcut – Two keys pressed at the same time. Usually the 'control' key (Ctrl), 'Alt' key, or 'Shift' key combined with a letter or number. For example to use 'Control-D', press 'Control', tap the 'D' key once firmly then take your finger off the 'Control' key.

keywords – Words that sum up your web site for being indexed in search engines. For example for a cosmetic site the key words might include beauty, lipstick, make-up, fashion, cosmetic and so on.

kick – To eject someone from a chat channel.

LAN – A local area network, a computer network usually located in one building or campus.

link – A hypertext phrase or image that calls up another web page when you click on it. Most web sites have lots of hyperlinks, or 'links' for short. These appear on the screen as buttons, images or bits of text (often underlined) that you can click on with your mouse to jump to another site on the world wide web.

Linux – A new widely and freely available operating system for personal computers, and a potentially serious challenger to Microsoft. It has developed a considerable following.

listserver – An automated email system whereby subscribers are able to receive and send email from other subscribers to the list.

log on/log off – To access/leave a network. In the early days of computing this literally involved writing a record in a log book. You may be asked to 'log on' to certain sites and particular pages. This normally means entering your user ID in the form of a name and a password.

lurk – The slang term used to describe reading a newsgroup's messages without actually taking part in that newsgroup. Despite the connotations of the word, it is a perfectly respectable activity on the internet.

macros – 'Macro languages' are used to automate repetitive tasks in Word processors.

mail server – A remote computer that enables you to send and receive emails. Your internet access provider will usually act as your mail server.

mailing list – A forum where messages are distributed by email to the members of the forum. The two types of lists are discussion and announcement. Discussion lists allow exchange between list members. Announcement lists are one-way only and used to distribute information such as news or humour. A good place to find mailing lists is Liszt (http://www.liszt.com). You can normally quit a mailing list by sending an email message to request removal.

marquee – A moving (scrolling) line of text on a web site, normally used for advertising purposes.

Media player – Software on a personal computer that will play sounds and images including video clips and animations.

metasearch engine – A site that sends a keyword search to many different search engines and directories so you can use many search engines from one place.

meta tags – The technical term for the keywords used in your web page code to help search engine software rank your site.

Mixmaster – An anonymous remailer that sends and receives email messages as packages of exactly the same size and often randomly varies the delay time between receiving and remailing to make interception harder.

modem – This is an internal or external piece of hardware plugged into your PC. It links into a standard phone socket, thereby giving you access to the internet. The word derives from MOdulator/DEModulator.

moderator – A person in charge of a mailing list, newsgroup or forum. The moderator prevents unwanted messages.

mpeg – or **mpg** – The file format used for video clips available on the internet. See

Glossary ....

also JPEG.

MP3 – An immensely popular audio format that allows you to download and play music on your computer. It compresses music to create files that are small yet whose quality is almost as good as CD music. See http://mpeg.org for further technical information, or the consumer web site www.mp3.com. At time of writing, MP4, even faster to download was being developed.

MUDs – Multi-User Dungeons, interactive chat-based fantasy world games. Popular in the early days of the internet, they are in now in decline with the advance of networked arcade games such as Quake and Doom.

navigate – To click on the hyperlinks on a web site in order to move to other web pages or internet sites.

net – A slang term for the internet. In the same way, the world wide web is often just called the web.

netiquette – Popular term for the unofficial rules and language people follow to keep electronic communication in an acceptably polite form.

Netmeeting – This Microsoft plug in allows a moving video picture to be contained within a web page. It is now integrated into Windows Media Player.

Netscape – After Microsoft's Internet Explorer, Netscape is the most popular browser software available for surfing the internet. An excellent browser, Netscape has suffered in the wake of Internet Explorer, mainly because of the success of Microsoft in getting the latter pre-loaded on most new PCs. Netscape Communicator comes complete with email, newsgroups, address book and bookmarks, plus a web page composer, and you can adjust its settings in all sorts of useful ways. Netscape was taken over by American Online for $4 billion.

nettie – Slang term for someone who likes to spend a lot of time on the internet.

newbie – Popular term for a new member of a newsgroup or mailing list.

newsgroup – A Usenet discussion group. Each newsgroup is a collection of messages, usually unedited and not checked by anyone ('unmoderated'). Messages can be placed within the newsgroup by anyone including you. It is rather like reading and sending public emails. The ever-growing newsgroups have been around for much longer than the world wide web, and are an endless source of information, gossip, news, entertainment, sex, politics, resources and ideas. The 50,000-plus newsgroups are collectively referred to as Usenet, and millions of people use it every day.

news reader – A type of software that enables you to search, read, post and manage messages in a newsgroup. It will normally be supplied by your internet service provider when you first sign up, or preloaded on your new computer. The best known are Microsoft Outlook, and Netscape Messenger.

news server – A remote computer (e.g. your internet service provider) that enables you to access newsgroups. If you cannot get some or any newsgroups from your existing news server, use your favourite search engine to search for 'open news servers' – there are lots of them freely available. When you have found one you like, add it to your news reader. The first time you do this, it may take 10 to 20 minutes to load the names of all the newsgroups onto your computer, but after that they open up in seconds whenever you want them.

nick – Nickname, – an alias you can give yourself and use when entering a chat channel, rather than using your real name.

Nominet – The official body for registering domain names in the UK (for example web sites whose name ends in .co.uk).

online – The time you spend linked via a modem to the internet. You can keep your phone bill down by reducing online time. The opposite term is offline.

open source software – A type of freely modifiable software, such as Linux. A definition and more information can be found at: www.opensource.org

OS – The operating system in a computer, for example MS DOS (Microsoft Disk Operating System), or Windows 95/98.

packet – The term for any small piece of data sent or received over the internet on your behalf by your internet service provider, and containing your address and the recipient's address. One email message for example may be transmitted as several different packets of information, reassembled at the other end to recreate the message.

password – A word or series of letters and numbers that enables a user to access a file, computer or program. A passphrase is a password made by using more than one word.

PC – Personal computer: not an Apple Mac.

Pentium – The name of a very popular microprocessor chip in personal computers, manufactured by Intel. The first Pentium IIIs were supplied with secret and unique personal identifiers, which ordinary people surfing the net were unwittingly sending out, enabling persons unknown to construct detailed user profiles. After a storm of protest, Pentium changed the technology so that this identifier could be disabled. If you buy or use a Pentium III computer you should be aware of this risk to your privacy when online.

PGP – Pretty Good Privacy. A proprietary method of encoding a message before transmitting it over the internet. With PGP, a message is first compressed then encoded with the help of keys. Just like the valuables in a locked safe, your message is safe unless a person has access to the right keys. Many governments (as in France today) would like complete access to people's private keys. New Labour wanted access to everyone's keys in the UK, but dropped the proposed legislation after widespread protests. Unlike in many countries, there is no general right to privacy in the UK.

ping – You can use a ping test to check the connection speed between your computer and another computer.

plug in – A type of (usually free and downloadable) software required to add some form of functionality to web page viewing. A well-known example is Macromedia Shockwave, a plug in which enables you to view animations.

PoP – Point of presence. This refers to the dial up phone numbers available from your ISP. If your ISP does not have a local point of presence (i.e. local access phone number), then don't sign up – your telephone bill will rocket because you will be charged national phone rates. All the major ISPs have local numbers covering the whole of the country.

portal site – Portal means gateway. It is a web site designed to be used as a 'home base' from which you can start your web experience each time you go online. Portals often serve as general information points and offer news, weather and other information that you can customise to your own needs. Yahoo! is a good example of a portal (http://www.yahoo.com). A portal site includes the one that loads into your browser each time you connect to the internet. It could for example be the front page of your internet service provider. Or you can set your browser to make it some other front page, for example a search engine such as Yahoo!, or even your own home page if you have one.

post, to – The common term used for sending ('posting') messages to a newsgroup. Posting messages is very like sending emails, except of course that they are public and everyone can read them. Also, newsgroup postings are archived, and can be read by anyone in the world years later. Because of this, many people feel more comfortable using an 'alias' (made-up name) when posting messages.

privacy – You have practically no personal privacy online. Almost every mouse click and key stroke you make while online is being electronically logged, analysed and possibly archived by internet organisations, government agencies, police or other surveillance services. You are also leaving a permanent trail of data on whichever computer you are using. But then, if you have nothing to hide you have nothing to fear. To explore privacy issues worldwide visit the authoritative Electronic Frontier Foundation web site at www.eff.org, and for the UK, www.netfreedom.org.

protocol – Technical term for the method by which computers communicate. A protocol is something that has been agreed and can be used between systems. For example, for viewing web pages your computer would use hypertext transfer protocol (http). For downloading and uploading files, it would use file transfer protocol (ftp). It's not something to worry too much about in ordinary life.

proxy – An intermediate computer or server, used for reasons of security.

Quicktime – A popular free software program from Apple Computers. It is designed to play sounds and images including video clips and animations on both Apple Macs and personal computers.

refresh, reload – The refresh or reload button on your browser toolbar tells the web page you are looking at to reload.

register – You may have to give your name, personal details and financial information to some sites before you can continue to use the pages. Site owners may want to produce a mailing list to offer you products and services. Registration is also used to discourage casual traffic.

registered user – Someone who has filled out an online form and then been granted permission to access a restricted area of a web site. Access is usually obtained by logging on, typically by entering a password and user name.

remailer – A remailer preserves your privacy by acting as a go-between when you browse or send email messages. An anonymous remailer is simply a computer connected to the internet that can forward an email message to other people after stripping off the header of the messages. Once a message is routed through an anonymous remailer, the recipient of that message, or anyone intercepting it, can no longer identify its origin.

RFC – Request for comment. RFCs are the way that the internet developers propose changes and discuss standards and procedures. See http://rs.internic.net.

RSA – One of the most popular methods of encryption, and used in Netscape browsers. See http://www.rsa.com.

router – A machine that direct internet data (network packets) from one place to another.

search engine – A search engine is a web site you can use for finding something on the internet. Popular search engines are big web sites and information directories in their own right. There are hundreds of them; the best known include Alta Vista, Excite, Google, Infoseek, Lycos and Yahoo!.

secure servers – The hardware and software provided so that people can use their credit cards and leave other details without the risk of others seeing them online. Your browser will tell you when you are entering a secure site.

secure sockets layer (SSL) – A standard piece of technology which ensures secure financial transactions and data flow over the internet.

security certificate – Information that is used by the SSL protocol to establish a secure connection. Security certificates contain information about who it belongs to, who it was issued by, some form of unique identification, valid dates, and an encrypted fingerprint that can be used to verify the contents of the certificate. In order for an SSL connection to be created both sides must have a valid security certificate.

server – Any computer on a network that provides access and serves information to other computers.

shareware – Software that you can try before you buy. Usually there is some kind of limitation such as an expiry date. To get the registered version, you must pay for the software, typically $20 to $40. A vast amount of shareware is now available on the internet.

Shockwave – A popular piece of software produced by Macromedia, which enables you to view animations and other special effects on web sites. You can download it free and in a few minutes from Macromedia's web site. The effects can be fun, but they slow down the speed at which the pages load into your browser window.

signature file – This is a little text file in which you can place your address details, for adding to email and newsgroup messages. Once you have created a signature file, it is appended automatically to your emails. You can of course delete or edit it.

Slashdot – One of the leading technology news web sites, found at: http://slashdot.org

smiley – A form of **emoticon** – .

snail mail – The popular term for the standard postal service involving post-persons, vans, trains, planes, sacks and sorting offices.

spam – The popular term for electronic junk mail – unsolicited and unwelcome email messages sent across the internet. The term comes from Monty Python. There are various forms of spam-busting software which you can now obtain to filter out unwanted email messages.

sniffer – A program on a computer system (usually an ISP's system) designed to collect information. Sniffers are often used by hackers to collect passwords and user names.

SSL – Secure socket layer, a key part of internet security technology.

subscribe – The term for accessing a newsgroup in order to read and post messages in the newsgroup. There is no charge, and you can subscribe, unsubscribe and resubscribe at will with a click of your mouse. Unless you post a message, no-one in the newsgroup will know that you have subscribed or unsubscribed.

surfing – Slang term for browsing the internet, especially following trails of links on pages across the world wide web.

sysop – Systems operator, someone rather like a moderator for example of a chat room or bulletin board service.

TCP/IP – Transmission control protocol/internet protocol, the essential technology of the internet. It's not normally something you need worry about.

telnet – Software that allows you to connect via the internet to a remote computer and work as if you were a terminal linked to that system.

theme – A term in web page design. A theme describes the general colours and graphics used within a web site. Many themes are available in the form of readymade templates.

thread – An ongoing topic in a Usenet newsgroup or mailing list discussion. The term refers to the original message on a particular topic, and all the replies and other messages which spin off from it. With news reading software, you can easily 'view thread' and thus read the related messages in a convenient batch.

traceroute – A program that traces the route from your machine to a remote system. It is useful if you need to discover a person's ISP, for example in the case of a spammer.

traffic – The amount of data flowing across the internet, to a particular web site, newsgroup or chat room, or as emails.

trojan horse – A program that seems to perform a useful task but is really a malevolent program designed to cause damage to a computer system.

uploading – The act of copying files from your PC to a server or other PC on the internet, for example when you are publishing your own web pages. The term is most commonly used to describe the act of copying HTML pages onto the internet via FTP.

UNIX – This is a computer operating system that has been in use for many years, and still is used in many larger systems. Most ISPs use it.

URL – Uniform resource locator the address of each internet page. For example, the URL of Internet Handbooks is http://www.internet-handbooks.co.uk

Usenet – The collection of well over 50,000 active newsgroups that make up a substantial part of the internet.

virtual reality – The presentation of a lifelike scenario in electronic form. It can be used for gaming, business or educational purposes.

virus – A computer program maliciously designed to cause havoc to people's computer files. Viruses can typically be received when downloading program files from the internet, or from copying material from infected disks. Even Word files can now be infected. You can protect yourself from the vast majority of them by installing some inexpensive anti-virus software, such as Norton, McAfee or Dr Solomon.

web authoring – Creating HTML pages to upload onto the internet. You will be a web author if you create your own home page for uploading onto the internet.

web client – Another term for a browser.

Webcrawler – A popular internet search engine used to find pages relating to specific keywords entered.

webmaster – Any person who manages a web site.

web page – Any single page of information you can view on the world wide web. A typical web page includes a unique URL (address), headings, text, images, and hyperlinks (usually in the form of graphic icons, or underlined text). One web page usually contains links to lots of other web pages, either within the same web site or elsewhere on the world wide web.

web rings – A network of interlinked web sites that share a common interest.

Whois – A network service that allows you to consult a database containing information about someone. A whois query can, for example, help to find the identity of someone who is sending you unwanted email messages.

Windows – The ubiquitous operating system for personal computers developed by Bill Gates and the Microsoft Corporation. The Windows 3.1 version was followed by Windows 95, further enhanced by Windows 98. Windows 2000 is the latest.

WWW – The world wide web. Since it began in 1994 this has become the most popular part of the internet. The web is now made up of more than a billion web pages of every imaginable description, typically linking to other pages. Developed by the British computer scientist, Tim Berners-Lee, its growth has been exponential and is set to continue so.

WYSIWYG – 'What you see is what you get.' If you see it on the screen, then it should look just the same when you print it out.

Yahoo! – Probably the world's most popular internet directory and search engine, and now valued on Wall Street at billions of dollars: http://www.yahoo.com

zip/unzip – Many files that you download from the internet will be in compressed format, especially if they are large files. This is to make them quicker to download. These files are said to be zipped or compressed. Unzipping these compressed files means returning them to their original size on receipt. Zip files have the extension '.zip' and are created (and unzipped) using WinZip or a similar popular software package.

Index

. . . .

Index...